Praise for
A Woman's Guide to Power, Presence and Protection

"*A Woman's Guide to Power, Presence, and Protection* is a timely look at empowerment. The authors walk us through 12 rules that lead to power as they show us the actual value of using and keeping power. Based on serious research, these are critical rules to enhance your work presence while maintaining control. Women can utilize this book to carve a path to a successful career and family life."
— Dr. Diane Hamilton, Business Behavioral Expert, author of *Cracking the Curiosity Code*

"Informs and inspires! Like having a prime seat at a life changing seminar."
— Silvina Moschini, CEO of SheWorks! and Executive Producer of Unicorn Hunters

"Corporate life has always been an uneven playing field for aspiring women, though following these brilliant rules will begin to change that… FINALLY!"
— Michael Feiner, Author of *The Feiner Points of Leadership*, former Professor of Columbia Business School

"This book is a MUST read for any woman in a leadership role or seeking to represent herself more effectively in any professional or personal space. The authors discuss 12 rules as a framework to not only facilitate but elevate voice, presence and agency and put into action servant and value-based leadership. This book gives women the tools to know themselves, to be themselves and rise successfully above gender biases, inequities and close existing gaps."
— Marcela Del Carmen, MD, MGH, President of the Massachusetts General Physicians Organization, Massachusetts General Hospital

"*A Woman's Guide to Power, Presence and Protection* provides the vital skills women need—leveraging their power, influence and organizational savvy to realize their success. This book is a must read for women, the men who support them and companies looking to win in today's e   my and competitive world."
— Nila Betof, PhD. COO, The Leaders Edge (retired)

"The authors have offered a practical and   lp women utilize their full power and pot   advice with numerous examples to help wo.   and gender-based expectations."
— Steve Milovich, Former Senior Vice Pre.   .man Resources, The Walt Disney Company, and President, Milovic . artners

"I could feel the warmth of these brilliant and successful women sharing their stories and vulnerabilities. The rules are very useful and actionable. I'm ready to start practicing today and to share them with the women (and men) around me!"
— Tanya Trejo, Women Affinity Group Board Member

"This book is a breakthrough, a landmark in supporting and encouraging women leaders. Recognizing that the game is different for women is not enough. We need insightful and practical guidance to help women recognize and unleash their incredible skills and power in the workplace. As the father of two working daughters, I celebrate this book and the opportunity it offers to help them gain the credit, respect and responsibility they deserve."
— Peter D. Gibbons, Former CEO of TireHub LLC

"A must-have guide for women as well as the men with whom they work. Powerful, practical with hundreds of gender-specific savvy, collaboration, self-promotion and protection tips you can use immediately."
— Ed Betof, EdD, WW, VP, Talent Management and CLO, BD (retired), President, Betof Associates, LLC

"My time with Marty on the 12 Rules gave me such deep insights into potentially self-defeating behaviors that I was engaging in without fully recognizing them at the time. Thanks to the 12 Rules I have really benefitted from looking at myself differently and accepting I could make improvements that would not only help my career—but that could also help me support others around me."
— Susan Morris, Chief Operations Officer, Albertsons Companies

"There is no more important talent strategy for a business than to attract, develop, and empower women. This book is an invaluable contribution to achieving those goals. Seldman's proven and practical tools and tips will help any woman enhance her effectiveness as a leader, grow her career, and effectively navigate the inevitable organizational politics with integrity. In addition, the experiences of three highly successful female business leaders provide real world perspective and validation of the tools as well as 9 inspirational stories of success. It is a must read for any aspiring female business leader."
— Mike White, Former CEO of Directv

"It may take until 2085 for women to achieve equal status with men in some leadership roles in the United States, according to estimates. If you don't want to wait that long, read this playbook and apply its 12 powerful rules today."
— Caroline Leach, Executive Coach and Former Fortune 100 Executive

"This book is required reading for any woman in business, and a blueprint for ensuring your power and full potential are unleashed. The proactive and protective skills are necessary to not only survive and thrive in business."
— Lyndsay Lord, Chief Human Resource Officer, DECA Dental

"This guide provides critical insights on impediments female leaders face in the business environment. At the same time, it provides practical steps on how to address these issues and level the playing field. CEOs and business leaders who take advantage of the 12 Rules will create a competitive advantage in their organizations and unlock the full potential of their teams."
— Dan Guill, Chief Executive Officer, Enlivant

"The important work presented by this book has extraordinary value and will have positive impact on any individual, organization and to society as a whole. This must read will equip the reader with practical tools to do better at all aspects of life, unleash one's raw potential, and become a stronger, better person."
— Tomer Harpaz, Former CEO, Sabra Dipping Company, LLC

"This refreshingly frank book's 12 Rules are each explained with real-life examples and augmented with CEO perspectives, all focused on issues that most often affect women leaders in the workplace. It mentors women leaders by equipping them with the tools they need to succeed with integrity and savvy while staying true to themselves."
— Mike O'Sullivan, General Counsel, Snap Inc.

"Phronesis! Once again Marty shares practical wisdom for navigating organizational life. This time he's partnered with some incredible senior female executives to share personal stories of how they have applied these principles to navigate more purposeful outcomes."
— Portia Green, Vice President, Organization Strategy, Talent Development, & Inclusion, Direct-to-Consumer, NBC Universal

"As always, Marty's narration is well researched, relatable and simple to read. The 12 rules, if understood and implemented, will enable organizations to offer equitable opportunities to female leaders based on their talent, contribution and potential."
— Omer Gajial, Senior Vice President of Pharmacy and Health, Albertsons Companies

A Woman's Guide to Power, Presence and Protection

To Erika,

all the best,

Marty Seldman

Feb 13, 2022

A Woman's Guide to Power, Presence and Protection

12 Rules for Gaining the Credit, Respect and Recognition You Deserve

Mónica Bauer, Marty Seldman, Paula Santilli and Jovita Thomas-Williams

Optimum Press

 Optimum Press

Optimum Press
A division of Optimum Associates, LLC
3115 NW 84th Terrace
Pembroke Pines, FL 33024
www.optimumassociates.com

For more information, visit www.AWomansGuidetoPower.com

Edited by Heather Rodino
Book design by Christy Day, www.constellationbookservices.com
Cover art by Atlas Studio

ISBN (paperback): 978-1-7350593-4-1
ISBN (ebook): 978-1-7350593-5-8

Library of Congress Control Number: 2022900041

Publisher's Cataloging-in-Publication data

Names: Bauer, Mónica, author. | Seldman, Marty, author. | Santilli, Paula, author. | Thomas-Williams, Jovita, author. Title: A woman's guide to power, presence and protection : 12 rules for gaining the credit , respect and responsibility you deserve / Mónica Bauer, Marty Seldman, Paula Santilli, Jovita Thomas-Williams. Description: Includes bibliographical references. | Pembroke Pines, FL: Optimum Press, 2022. Identifiers: LCCN: 2022900041 | ISBN: 978-1-7350593-4-1 (paperback) | 978-1-7350593-5-8 (ebook) Subjects: LCSH Women in business. | Leadership. | Success in business. | Self-actualization (Psychology) | BISAC BUSINESS & ECONOMICS / Women in Business | BUSINESS & ECONOMICS / Careers / General | BUSINESS & ECONOMICS / Mentoring & Coaching
Classification: LCC HD6054 .B38 2022 | DDC 650.1082--dc23

Printed in the United States of America

To my beloved dad, John.
— Mónica Bauer

To Evelyn Bailey.
— Marty Seldman

To Matilde, my mom.
— Paula Santilli

To my beloved son, Alan, the center of my universe and light of my life.
— Jovita Thomas-Williams

Contents

OVERVIEW

Welcome. To start, we would like to provide you with a roadmap to what we hope will be an enjoyable, productive journey.

Chapter 1: Empowering You, Empowering Her

Here Mónica presents our key themes and core vision:

- Equipping women with the insights and skills to gain the power, impact, and influence they deserve.
- Then, women using their platform to support and lift up women at all levels of society.

She presents a compelling case for the benefits to organizations, families, and society when women occupy more leadership positions.

Chapter 2: Patterns Across Boundaries

An inspirational aspect of the book is that, as a way to illustrate the rules in action, it features the stories of nine successful female leaders from around the world. Mónica selected and interviewed them because, in addition to their achievements, they devote a considerable amount of time (in some cases all of their time) to supporting other women.

In this chapter, Mónica shares her observations about things this diverse group of women has in common.

Chapter 3: Introduction to the 12 Rules

The 12 Rules are founded on the research of Deborah Tannen (gender communication) and Kelly Reineke (power and communication) and Marty's extensive coaching experience with 650 women. They have been further enhanced by insights gained from Paula and Mónica, who have conducted 12 Rules workshops across Latin America, and Jovita, who has led seminars for women of color.

This chapter describes four key areas where many women are at a disadvantage relative to the pace and progress of their careers.

Chapters 4–15 (The 12 Rules)

These chapters contain dozens of tips, techniques, and skills that are easy to learn and can be implemented on day one. There are **proactive skills,** designed to ensure that your organization makes informed, fair decisions based on an accurate picture of your contributions, talent, and potential. There are also **protective skills,** which are unfortunately necessary to deal with marginalization, "gaslighting," power plays, sabotage, and attempts to steal credit.

For some of us, most importantly, there are systems for maintaining the necessary self-care and "healthy selfishness" to set ourselves up for success.

The chapters are enriched with:

- The CEO's Perspective: Paula shares her learnings from her career journey to CEO.

- Leadership profiles: inspirational and educational life stories from Mónica's interviews with nine international leaders.

- Case studies based on real situations from Marty's coaching practice.

- Self-Assessments: At the end of each chapter you'll take an assessment, which will guide you to a behavior change/skill acquisition action plan.

Chapter 16: The 12 Rules for Women of Color

Jovita has spent 30-plus years as a top-level human resources executive in some of the US's largest corporations. She has had a seat at the table for thousands of talent reviews and has mentored and trained hundreds of women. In this chapter she focuses on the unique challenges facing women of color in the workplace. She shares her insights and suggestions for customizing the 12 Rules and builds a case for why they may be even more necessary for women of color.

Chapter 17: Men, Our Key Allies

Going beyond the fact that many men could also benefit from applying some of the 12 Rules, Mónica explains the specific ways male allies can mentor, sponsor, and support women.

CHAPTER 1

Empowering You, Empowering Her

Today more than ever, the global economy needs to recover. A crucial element of the solution is unleashing the economic power of women. It's critical to increase awareness of opportunity to achieve success.

We know this is not easy. Women face many challenges in their social, economic, and work environments, and we hope this book will provide insights into overcoming these obstacles. We aim to raise women's self-confidence by providing them with the tools they need to stimulate their personal development and close the gender gap. We want to inspire you, encourage you, and help you and the women around you. That's how we will achieve a positive impact.

The central idea of the twelve rules is that women should better understand their power, feel comfortable using it, and never give it away. This book tells the stories of nine women who have put these rules into practice. Before we list in detail the skills you can develop to increase your work success, let us start by explaining why it is vital to encourage women's participation. The truth is that women are often unaware of or minimize their contributions to the companies they work for and their communities. There are still taboos against being more vocal about your achievements and impact.

Additionally, our sensitivity as women can make us less likely to talk about our achievements. We feel that doing so is arrogant or will make someone else feel bad. Other times we experience the infamous impostor syndrome where we don't feel we're genuinely deserving. We downplay our greatness. To take charge of our careers, however, we need to promote our achievements. Thus, a fundamental step in proving women's value to the world is that we need to own our accomplishments and track records while encouraging other women to do the same.

The social impact produced by the increase of women in the working world is incredible and extends out in concentric circles, first to the women themselves as individuals, then to their families, to the companies where they work, and finally to their communities.[1]

Furthermore, the McKinsey Global Institute calculates that, if women's equality were to advance on a global scale, $12 trillion could be added to GDP growth by 2025.[2]

In short, when women work, economies grow,[3] businesses grow,[4] and communities strengthen. Women's economic empowerment is one of the most critical factors for achieving equality. When women work, it creates prosperity for all.

Many women have been socialized from a young age to comply with both implicit and explicit gender-based expectations. Gender roles and the pressure to conform to them vary across regions, religions, and households. Generally, these expectations are firmly embedded in the culture and carry over into the workplace. Girls in many cultures are taught obedience to authority, to be nurturing and polite. Value may be placed on women's sole aspiration to be wives and mothers. Many are culturally driven to find a partner who will provide while they raise the children. In many places, these cultural gender role expectations are further reinforced through laws or religion.

Some decision-makers believe that women will be less committed to their jobs because they will want to have families and children. Others expect that women will leave their jobs to take care of their families since their income is considered merely a supplement to their spouse's.

Although women comprise half of the world's working-age population, there is still a significant difference between the number of women in the workforce and the number of men.

In the United States, women have made much progress in the labor market. Women's participation in the formal economy has been an essential factor in the growth of the US economy over the last 125 years. Despite that progress, women are still being left behind in leadership positions, earnings, and underrepresentation overall. This reality has significantly affected minority and marginalized women. COVID has complicated this reality and remains a striking setback.

The economic impacts of COVID on women in the workforce are manifold. From 2019 to 2020, 7 percent of working American women left the workforce.[5] Globally, women lost $800 billion in income, which is equal to the "combined wealth of 98 countries," according to Oxfam.[6] Moreover, the pandemic revealed how women are the "shock absorbers" who bridge the care gap that became either unavailable because of school closures or too expensive because of job losses.[7]

Women in the American Workforce

Starting in the late 19th century and ever-expanding in the 20th century, women's role in the economy grew steadily. This growth rate wasn't a straight line upwards, though, as women's working lives have always been affected by family roles, discrimination, technology, and global events. The first working women[8] in the US were usually poor, uneducated, single women who worked in manufacturing or as domestic employees. This shifted just before WWI, with the growth of women working in clerical and teaching positions. This was due in part to compulsory education laws requiring students to attend school until age 14. From the 1930s to the 1950s, more married women began working—primarily because more women were finishing high school. In 1890, only 8 percent of working women were married, and by 1950, 25 percent of working women were married.[9]

By 1970, 50 percent of single women and 40 percent of married women were actively engaged in the labor force.[10] Then from the 1970s to the early 21st century, women's view of our own work-life balance shifted as we began to plan for long careers "unaffected" by marriage or children. As a result, women began to invest more in our education and to prepare for higher-level careers.[11] Since 1988, women have outnumbered men on college campuses.[12] Since 1980, women have earned one-third of all law degrees[13] and have been one-third of all medical students.[14] In 1980, no women were in the executive ranks in Fortune 100 companies, but by 2001, 11 percent of leadership was female.[15] By the 1990s, 74 percent of women were working (compared with 93 percent of men).[16] Now, women earn nearly 60 percent of all college undergraduate degrees and master's degrees,[17] 38 percent of MBAs, and 48 percent of specialized master's degrees.[18]

Despite this progress, women have not moved up into prominent positions of power at a rate that would mirror this progress. At the turn of the century, the advances in women's participation in the labor force leveled out and then began to decline. At the current rate of change, some estimates say it will take until 2085 for women to achieve equal status with men in some leadership roles in the United States.

COVID's Impact on Women's Participation in the Workforce

Despite the slow progress just described, women have been disproportionately affected by the pandemic, both at home and at work. Inequalities are more apparent. One in four women left the workforce or downshifted their careers (compared to one in five men), and of the women making this choice, working mothers, women in senior management positions, and black women have been more affected. One in six women of color are facing food shortages in the US because of the pandemic.[19] When there were children under the age of ten in the household, 10 percent more women considered leaving compared to men.[20] According to the International Labor Organization (ILO), more women than men lost their jobs, and in most cases, they haven't returned to work.[21]

Moreover, women work in the hardest-hit sectors of the economy including: hospitality and food service, business and administration, manufacturing, and retail.[22] Worldwide, that's 41 percent of total female formal sector employment.[23] Oxfam says that women lost $800 billion in income worldwide in 2020, and this is almost certainly an underestimate as it doesn't include the millions of women working in the informal sector.[24]

One cause of this workplace regression is the reality of childcare and domestic work worldwide, which is estimated at $10.8 trillion annually.[25] Back in 2018, the ILO estimated that there are 1.9 billion children, including 800 million children under the age of six, that need childcare.[26] Women provide a disproportionate amount of all childcare.

In 2018, 606 million women of working age were unavailable for employment owing to childcare responsibilities, compared to just 41 million men.[27] COVID intensified the care crisis when 90 percent of countries closed schools to reduce the risk of spread of the virus, leaving much of the burden of care gap to women. Further, as national budgets tighten, there are often cuts to services for child care, domestic violence, and maternal, sexual, reproductive, and mental health—which disproportionately affect women, especially racial minorities, women with disabilities, indigenous women, immigrants, refugees, and sexual and gender minorities. Economic recovery from COVID will have to address some of these structural inequalities.

Unleashing the Economic Power of Women to Drive Growth and Recovery

The COVID-19 pandemic caused a massive economic recession. Global growth was predicted to be 7 percent, but in reality, it was just 4.9 percent.[28] In 2021, the growth rate is projected to be just 5.4 percent, which will result in GDPs that are nearly six percentage points lower than previous projections. Deploying women's full potential is fundamental to economic recovery. When the 2008 recession struck, women helped push the US economy back up—so much so that some economists have even called it the country's first female recession.[29]

Moreover, it is important to point out that companies really do benefit from having women in their workforce. The Center for Creative Leadership analyzed companies on the list of Fortune 500—the 500 most important companies in the world—and discovered that those that include greater representation of women are financially superior to those with a lesser degree of female involvement. In addition, a study carried out by the Peterson Institute for International Economy and the EY Study Center shows that companies with at least 30 percent of their top management positions occupied by women report 15 percent more benefits.[30] Increasing the number of women in executive positions generates a 28 percent higher added economic value for the business and increases profit margins by 55 percent. This is due, in part, because teams that include both genders register more sales and profits than those dominated by men. Diversity promotes innovation, which in turn is linked to greater profitability. Also, the style of feminine leadership and its influence on teamwork increase the levels of productivity.

Social Impact Produced by Women in the Workforce

Women leaders who remain in the workforce have really stepped up to the challenge. We are doing more than men in similar positions to support our teams. Employees are more likely to report that their manager has supported or helped them in the past year *if* their manager is a woman. Studies show that women in similar positions to men support their teams more—for example, "by helping team members navigate work–life challenges, ensuring that their workloads are manageable, and checking in on their overall well-being."[31] Moreover, women leaders spend more time on diversity, equity, and inclusion (DEI) work, which means that more female leaders are showing up as allies to women of color. All of these factors contribute to overall well-being by increasing happiness and decreasing burnout—which makes employees less likely to leave their jobs.

Research shows, research shows that the more women are represented at higher levels, the more often the gender gap closes within the workplace and in boardrooms.[32] When there are more women in positions of leadership, more women are promoted across sectors—though women are still likely to receive a lower wage increase from those promotions.[33] Matsa and Miller (2011)[34] and Bell (2005)[35] both found evidence that women help women at the highest levels of major US corporations. The benefits include increases in female board representation, which are then followed in later years by greater female representation at the CEO and top executive level and smaller gender pay gaps among top executives.

In short, empowered women are empowering women. As a gender, we've surmounted many obstacles, but many remain as outlined by the shortages of women in positions of power, the pay gap, and the impact of a pandemic on women's role as caregiver for children.

CHAPTER 2

Patterns Across Boundaries

The starting point of our book is the belief that empowered women can and do empower other women. Diversity is a proven indicator of company competitiveness, so we also wanted to be sure that a diversity of voices was reflected in the stories in this book. They were chosen not only for their leadership but because of their commitment to other women. Here is what we learned and observed from those interviews.

To illustrate the 12 Rules, we interviewed nine successful women with diverse backgrounds from the US, Ukraine, Philippines, Argentina, Nepal, Nicaragua, Kenya, and Israel. We chose these women not only because of their remarkable trajectories but because all of them have a strong common conviction: that empowered women should empower other women. This is our key call to action in the book: Use the 12 Rules to accelerate your career growth and empower yourself, and make sure that, along the way, you bring other women with you. That virtuous cycle will have an impressive impact on our workplaces, our communities, and ultimately in the development of a more diverse, inclusive, and equal world.

As the authors of this book, it has been our privilege to capture the values and passion of these women so that their voices will resonate and reverberate in the hearts and minds of our readers.

Despite the diversity of the women we interviewed, we were able to draw several commonalities among them that we'd like to share with you:

Women are resilient, hardworking, and determined.

Gendered vulnerability means that women (and girls) are disproportionately affected by risks due to cultural or social norms, disasters, climate change, disasters, and violence. Women around the world rise with resilience, hard work, and determination, but too many women are not aware of their own resilience. Fostering women's leadership and resilience building facilitates self-confidence and empowerment that can transform power relations at home and at work. This is the key to overcoming barriers that have traditionally excluded women from leadership. Women rise to the occasion, and these stories outline the transformative changes that women have experienced. When women share their struggles and successes, they help other women build resilience that can be applied to their own lives.

Women put a lot of passion into their work.

At work, women leverage their passion, practicality, and personal fulfillment. The importance of passion was apparent when times were difficult during the pandemic. Passion is contagious, and passionate women inspire and energize the workplace. The result is better team performance because those teams then engage in more creative problem-solving and become more resilient. A passionate leader builds her team's spirit by setting goals that the team can work toward together, creating a culture of collaboration and seeking out new challenges as opportunities to learn. The women in these stories demonstrate that passion is a vital element that produces extraordinary results.

Women have a strong drive to support their communities and leave a legacy.

Women leaders expressed compassion and empathy for their subordinates, as many knew what it was to have to balance a caretaker role with full-time work. Women drew from their own lived experiences of exclusion or marginalization to be better leaders. Shared experiences like this informed pandemic decision-making and how the workplace could be more flexible but still productive. Beyond the factor of basic human decency, the women in our stories are driven to encourage others to be their best selves. Women are championing other women at work, which is leveling the playing field. This is a legacy—an enduring record of who we are, what we stand for, and the impact we've had, and many women have chosen a legacy of empowering other women.

Women aren't generally good at self-promoting.

The evidence is clear: Women don't assess their performance, ability, and potential at the same level as men who perform equally well. Talking about our accomplishments and abilities is tricky for a number of reasons. As girls, we were conditioned not to brag, and as a result, we assume that our hard work will speak for itself. School reinforces this notion because when we're good, quiet students, our work does speak for itself. Women tend to be judged more harshly (even by other women) for self-promoting. Women also face double standards that men don't. For example, confidence and assertiveness are acceptable characteristics for men, but those qualities go against societal expectations for women. This likeability penalty makes it more challenging for women to assert themselves. The stories in this book explore women's struggles, and successes, with self-promotion.

Women struggle with power—either giving it away or feeling uncomfortable using it.

Many of the women we interviewed struggled with power. In some cases, it was because they were raised and taught the value of obedience. In other cases, they felt comfortable using their power until they reached a certain level in the organization, and then, due to factors such as fear, guilt, high levels of approval and others, they started giving it away. Additionally, some of the women we interviewed did not trust their own abilities to handle risks. The stories in this book exemplify women who've had many of the same fears and faced the same obstacles but took courage and believed in themselves to overcome them.

Women have been affected by the COVID-19 pandemic.

In addition to the direct health consequences that many families have faced, the COVID-19 pandemic shifted and/or damaged the work-life balance and well-being of many women. Women—especially women of color—were hit harder by redundancies, job losses, or temporary unemployment measures. When women remained employed, they often had to combine the home office with homeschooling, in addition to household work and other childcare duties. All of these affected women's feelings of control and even self-worth. Many women felt more fear now than they did before COVID. The pandemic has made them more risk averse. Women are rebuilding their lives in this complex environment, and resilience empowers women to take the next steps in regaining balance as they become agents for change.

Women feel that economic empowerment is key.

Most of the women we interviewed felt that economic empowerment has been a key enabler for them to feel free and decide what they want to do with their lives. Empowered women shape families, companies, economies, and countries. Studies show that there's a positive connection between women's empowerment and a country's social and economic growth because when women work, economies grow. Economic empowerment is also the central pillar for realizing gender equality on a broad scale.

Women foster the power of the pack.

When women rise through the ranks, there is a strong correlation with paying it forward by helping future talent navigate the course. Research shows that women who support other women are more successful, and overall, we found a common spirit of women trying to help other women. There's a huge sense of sorority, and when more women are at the proverbial table, their collective power is stronger. Women are amplifying other women, and the results are extraordinary. In this book, women share their stories and journeys as a means to help break old patterns.

We welcome you to join us. These stories and rules are for everyone, so we hope that you will use these rules to be even better at what you do. We hope these stories inspire you and help you grow into your full potential as a leader. As you rise, remember: Empowered women empower women.

CHAPTER 3

Introduction to the 12 Rules

The foundation for the 12 Rules consists of the research on gender communication by linguistics professor Deborah Tannen, Ph. D ("You Just Don't Understand"), studies on the impact of power differences on communication by Kelly Reineke, Ph. D. (Ph. D. Dissertation), and insights gained from Marty's 35-year executive coaching process. The concepts and skills have been enhanced by Paula and Mónica, who have taught the 12 Rules to dozens of women's groups throughout Latin America, and Jovita's seminars on the 12 Rules for Women of Color.

Since 1986 I've coached about 2,000 leaders; approximately 650 of them have been women. This platform revealed crucial real-world information about career journeys and progression.

By tracking careers over long periods, I was able to see who reached their full potential, who plateaued, and who derailed.

As a result of thousands of internal conversations with senior leaders and Human Resource partners, I saw patterns of feedback and perceptions that disadvantaged women.

My key takeaways that formed the basis of the 12 Rules were:

- There is no guarantee that your hard work and achievements will lead to the rewards, recognition, and responsibilities you deserve.
- There are four areas where, in general, women are at a disadvantage to men with regard to career advancement.
- There are easy-to-learn and easy-to-use skills and techniques (the 12 Rules) that create a more even playing field.

The 12 Rules are based on a reality of corporate life. When your organization is conducting talent reviews or discussing the possibility of your advancement, you are not in the room. The objective of the 12 Rules is that, on that day, the company will make an informed, accurate decision based on your talent, contributions, and potential.

Female Advantages

Before we focus on the areas at work where women may be at a disadvantage or vulnerable, let's look at some of the research about female leadership advantages.

In the last 10 years, with the accelerating pace of change and increase in complexity, it's clear we live in a world where not only does no one person have all the answers, no one has all the information. Leaders who create a culture that encourages full participation tap into more of the knowledge and creativity of their teams. The research is clear that it is in an organization's best interest to increase the representation of female leaders.

> "Women-operated venture-backed, high-tech companies
> generated 12 percent higher annual revenues, using, on average,
> one-third less capital."
> **Cindy Padnos**, venture capitalist

> "Workplaces that are evenly split along gender lines
> are more productive and help the company's financial
> performance, compared to offices that lack gender diversity."
> **MIT research**

> "Women score higher than men on four out of five
> measures of Emotional Intelligence: Self Awareness,
> Self-Regulation, Empathy, and Social Skills. In the fifth measure,
> Self-Motivation, male-female scores are equal."
> **Lois Frankel, PhD**, *Nice Girls Don't Get the Corner Office*

> "More women in leadership positions correlates
> with stronger financial returns."
> **McKinsey & Co./Catalyst**

The evidence not only points to women's increased productivity and performance but also illuminates women's leadership advantages. Those higher emotional intelligence scores translate to leaders who excel at collaboration and building cohesive, engaged teams.

So, with these advantages, why is the path to entry and career progression still so difficult?

Disadvantages/Vulnerabilities

Bias and Privilege

In earlier chapters we have discussed cultural bias and barriers that severely disadvantage women. In addition to these challenges, women deal with other perceptions in the workplace as they are evaluated for leadership positions.

Catherine Rampell describes this as navigating the "narrow path."

1. Don't be "pushy," "bossy," or too aggressive, **BUT** don't be meek, weak, or too nice.

2. Don't be so emotional, dramatic, sensitive, **BUT** don't be so restrained or cold.

3. Don't focus so much on your career at the expense of your family, don't be a poor role model for work-life balance, **BUT** don't ask for generous maternity leave or carve outs for family responsibility.

4. Don't push for a raise or promotion, trust the company, **BUT** know your worth and ask for what you deserve.

5. Pay attention to how you are dressed so you don't look "frumpy," **BUT** don't overfocus on your looks because you will appear vain and superficial.

In the introduction we stated our goal in writing this book is to reduce inequality and to promote fairness and a more even playing field. In providing the 12 Rules, we will reveal how women can thrive and advance despite these conditions.

But first we need to share what we have learned about other types of disadvantages and vulnerabilities that many women share.

Male/Female Differences

Anytime anyone writes about male/female differences, you will hear these types of remarks:

"I'm a woman, and I'm not like that."

"I know men who have more of the female characteristics."

So before we introduce the four male/female differences that can disadvantage women in the workplace, we have a couple of caveats. When we describe a male/female difference, for example, self-promotion, and we say that on average men brag more than women and are more comfortable with self-promotion than women, we are *not* saying all men brag and *no* men struggle with self-promotion, or that *all* women are held back by a lack of effective self-promotion.

So what are these male/female differences that slow or derail women's careers?

1. Attitudes toward power
2. Effective self-promotion
3. Executive presence
4. Self-care/healthy selfishness

As you read about these differences and how each of them creates disadvantages for some women, note the ultimate irony. All four of these areas point to the strengths, right values, and good intentions of women. How can these good things lead to disadvantages and vulnerability?

- Strengths can be overused.
- Strengths can be used in the wrong situation.
- Overdeveloped strengths often lead to underdevelopment in other areas.

So trust, politeness, collaboration, humility, cooperation, generosity, and fairness are traits that in the wrong situation or dealing with the wrong person can actually work against you.

Attitudes Toward Power

Psychologist David McClelland once described two approaches to power that he labeled "Power With" and "Power Over."

Power With leaders utilize a noncoercive, shared version of power with their teams. They prefer to influence, persuade, and inspire others, and rely on their ability to reconcile and align various interests.

In 1998 when I was facilitating a seminar on these subjects with Women Unlimited, I asked the group Machiavelli's famous question, "Is a great leader loved or feared?" One woman replied, "Why would any leader want to be feared?" Research supports this anecdote, in that many women are attracted to the Power With model.

I remember a female CEO being asked about power, and she said she doesn't often use the word and would rather motivate people and model key leadership values.

The research also reveals that Power With leaders are able to engage and empower their teams. Their meetings are more likely to result in informed decision-making and aligned execution.

So, as the expression goes, "What's not to like?"

If Power With leaders are fortunate enough to work with leaders like themselves, their career path can be relatively smooth. If, however, a Power With leader has to regularly deal with a Power Over person, they can be exposed to a variety of risks.

Power Over leaders view the world through the lens of power. They often seek decision-making rights ("I'm the decider") and power over others. When they meet you, evaluating your talent and potential is secondary to estimating your power. They ask themselves:

"Does she have power?"

"Does she have powerful allies?"

"Is she naive, trusting, or reluctant to use her power?"

The answers to these questions determine how they will treat you (not returning phone calls, coming late to your meetings, not sharing information, and so on). They can be very comfortable with dominance and intimidation. If, for example, you gave them feedback that someone is afraid of them, that news can actually make them feel warm inside.

Power Over leaders love the word *power* and often use expressions and jokes that relate to it.

"If you're not the lead dog, the view never changes."

"The Golden Rule: the person with the gold makes the rule."

"They will find out fast there is a new sheriff in town"

Plus, they may make lots of references to "punishing" others or "playing hardball."

Of course, the Power Over approach comes in degrees, and of course, not all men are Power Over leaders. However, study after study shows that men are attracted to power and are comfortable using it.

Many women prefer the Power With approach and may be ambivalent about using their power, and they're often not equipped to deal with a Power Over boss, peer, or direct report. By expecting others to share your values and "play the game" like you do, you might be too slow to recognize how you are being undermined or marginalized. If you don't see it coming, don't anticipate and predict Power Over behavior, you won't be able to protect yourself or your team. This can have the unfortunate result of negating years of hard work and also allowing less-deserving people to be elevated in organizations.

What Power Over leaders can do to someone they are **not** afraid of:

- Take credit for ideas/accomplishments
- Assign blame when things go wrong
- Marginalize
- Publicly criticize
- Sabotage (withholding information, resources)
- Demote/derail

Several of the 12 Rules you will be learning will prepare you to quickly recognize when you are engaged with a Power Over person and to use strategies, skills, and your network to make sure you advance your ideas and your career.

Effective Self-Promotion

Shonda Rhimes, the creator (along with her Shondaland partner, Betsy Beers) of hit TV shows *Grey's Anatomy, How to Get Away with Murder,* and *Scandal,* recently received a distinguished industry award for her achievements. Standing in front of the audience to accept her award, she opened her remarks in the following way: "I totally deserve this award." Wow! Fantastic to hear. I loved it, and if more women were able to do this, I would not be including a section on self-promotion.

But my experience coaching and training thousands of women, as well as the experiences of coaches and authors like Lois Frankel, Nila Betof, Deborah Tannen, and Sally Helgesen and Marshall Goldsmith (authors of *How Women Rise*), points toward many women struggling with this issue.

Some women have a low need for attention and visibility and prefer to rely on fairness, believing that their results will speak for themselves and that ultimately the best ideas and best people will advance. Others, who find it difficult to achieve the right level of self-promotion, deal with a form of self-censorship. They fear being perceived as "conceited," "full of themselves," too ambitious, pursuing a personal agenda, or not being a "team player."

Either of these tendencies increases the risk that a woman will not get the credit or recognition she deserves.

Risk 1: Being Underestimated

The reality of organizational life is that the people who make decisions about your career are almost always incredibly busy. This means that incidents, "sound bites," and impressions from a meeting or a conference can form perceptions that rarely get checked out. Also, when leaders acquire power, they often pride themselves on sizing up people quickly. If you combine this with the fact that when key decision makers in your organization sit around a table to discuss your future, *you are not in the room!* You can't add to the conversation that you are a strategic thinker, that you created XYZ product two years ago, that you do look around corners, that you predicted the trend in our after-market sales. And yes, that you do have experience running a P&L; you did it successfully at your previous company.

So without a clear intention, and some effective language and skills, there is no guarantee your organization will make an informed decision about your contributions, talent, or potential.

Risk 2: Stolen Credit

Being underestimated is serious enough, but it gets worse because risk 1 invites risk 2.

There are often people in organizations who survive or even thrive although they are not as competent or don't work as hard as their peers.

How do they do it? First of all, they are very aware that busy decision makers may form impressions on limited contacts. They are also keen to observe the limited number of people who have access to, and influence on, key decision makers.

The final object of their study is you. If they notice that you don't seek visibility, that you rarely put your "handprint" on your work or tend to trust that the system will eventually recognize you, you become an enticing target.

Sometimes they will simply claim the idea or success. They may write an internal paper about it or give talks, discussing the work internally or externally. Other times they may use access to the decision maker or his or her network to "manage the airwaves" behind the scenes.

"I'm so glad that Sally finally listened to me because you can see we are really having an impact on market share."

"What do you mean?"

"Well, originally Sally was reluctant to go in this direction, but I pushed her to do a pilot. When that was successful, she came on board with this approach."

Of course, Sally is totally unaware of this conversation but is definitely puzzled by the absence of recognition for her recent success. I wish I could tell you this kind of stealing credit doesn't happen. I wish I could tell you the way the person framed Sally's initial reluctance would be challenged or checked out, that this gambit wouldn't work or even backfire. But sadly, I've seen this happen over and over, robbing leaders like Sally of the credit they and their teams deserve.

The rules you will learn about effective self-promotion are not designed for you to start bragging, exaggerating your accomplishments, or creating false impressions. They simply have one goal: that when your organization is making decisions about your future, they are fully aware of your contributions, abilities, and potential to add value.

As you can now see, without intention, skill, and overcoming some internal inhibitions, there is no guarantee this will happen.

Executive Presence

We convince by our presence. —Walt Whitman

If we come back to that talent review where people are sitting around the table deciding whether you are ready to take on more responsibility, a term that often is injected into the discussion is *executive presence*.

"How does she measure up in terms of executive presence?"

It can mean different things in different organizations and can refer to perceptions of gravitas, confidence, or forcefulness.

Because these perceptions are subjective, they are influenced by many verbal and nonverbal factors, such as posture, stance, eye contact, handshake, voice level, nervous mannerisms, facial expressions, types of humor, and so on.

Why do I bring executive presence into our discussion of male/female differences that can disadvantage women?

1. Whether we think it should be or not, executive presence is often a deciding factor in who gets promoted.

2. Executive presence is often seen through a male "lens" or framework. A comparable example I've experienced is watching US leaders go to countries like Thailand or Japan and use a US-centric "scorecard" for evaluating leadership, confidence, and toughness. I've seen many examples in my coaching practice where using the US definitions leads to underestimating Thai and Japanese leaders.

3. If women are not aware of how executive presence is defined in their organization, they may unintentionally lower their perceived presence and impact.

Here are some examples we will be focusing on: being too polite, smiling at the wrong time, being deferential, seeking approval, using self-deprecating humor, overapologizing, using tentative language, using a soft voice, shying away from public conflict, and allowing oneself to be marginalized in a meeting.

In addition, it's important to get feedback about your posture, stance, eye contact, handshake, voice composure, and vocabulary.

Healthy Selfishness

The quickest way for me to alert you to how this difference acutely disadvantages many women is to share the results of a recent study about "volunteering" in organizations.

The research examined who volunteers, how much, and what types of activities they volunteered for. The results showed clear male/female differences in these activities.

Women tended to say yes to volunteering for more activities (meetings, projects, trips, mentoring, additional responsibilities, and so on); they believed these efforts would help the organization, and they often didn't inform senior management about what they had done.

Men tend to say no more often; they were more selective in what they signed up for. Mostly they committed their time to projects that were a priority or of interest to people in power. And they were intentional about finding ways to inform senior management about their actions.

This volunteering (saying yes too quickly) is one of the main reasons, in my coaching practice and leadership seminars, I encounter dedicated, unselfish women who are overcommitted, "crazy busy," and can appear overwhelmed. There can be a variety of reasons for this difference: a difficulty saying no, a high need for approval, wanting to be a "team player," or simply believing that the organization would benefit from their actions.

Here is a recent example: After I gave a talk on the 12 Rules to women lawyers in Mexico, a participant reached out to me. She said that as the only female partner in her firm, the other partners often requested that she participate in meetings with their clients. So although she has small children and often would have to drive considerable distances, she would often say yes.

After hearing about the 12 Rules (particularly healthy selfishness, the "scorecard" for getting promoted, and "everything you say yes to, you say no to something else"), she realized she was undermining her chances for success at the firm. The parent company, a worldwide law firm, evaluated all partners based on their clients and fees they generated. She was helping the other partners, possibly helping the firm, but putting herself at an almost insurmountable disadvantage.

Recently KPMG completed a national survey of 2,000 women who work in corporate settings and found similar results: "First, it helps to understand the kinds of behaviors in which women are most likely to engage. As noted, these behaviors tend to benefit their company or their group and are less likely to raise their profile or achieve a personal benefit." (2019 KPMG Women's Leadership Study)

The cumulative results are definitely career limiting. If you are late on assignments, let some things fall through the cracks, or look disorganized or stressed, are you going to be perceived as a candidate for a promotion or more responsibility?

Assuming a male and female candidate had the same education, intelligence, and talent but differed in this one aspect of volunteering, whom would you bet on to go further in their career?

Mental health professionals have found that people who have difficulty saying no have higher levels of depression and anxiety.

So, we are going to focus on skills for how to say no and still be a team player, how to set boundaries on your personal and professional time, and how to make your needs and self-care a priority. This is what we refer to as developing "healthy selfishness."

It's useful to remember three famous maxims about how you spend your time:

1. *If you don't have a plan for your time, someone else will.* Other people make requests for your time that meet their agenda. Do they align with yours?

2. *We train other people how to treat us.* If people notice you have a hard time saying no, expect more of them to be asking for your time.

3. *Everything you say yes to, you say no to something else.* When you agree to spend time on "nice to do" activities, you may not get to do:

   - Strategic reflection
   - Key networking
   - A workout
   - Spending time on a relationship

Following the rules of healthy selfishness will allow you to do things that are good for the organization, your career, and your overall well-being.

Summary

As you have read about these differences and disadvantages, you have probably noticed that not all of them apply to you. That's good. Breathe a sigh of relief and congratulate yourself, but please still learn about all 12 Rules. Our reasoning is that these disadvantages are so common that even if they don't all apply to you, you will encounter a female colleague, direct report, mentee, niece, or daughter who could benefit from your guidance in one of these areas.

Self-Reflection

Please take a moment to look back over your career and perhaps your personal life and note your experiences with these issues.

1. Attitudes Toward Power
   - Power With versus Power Over
   - Experiences with Power Over leaders
   - Dealing with marginalization, power plays, stolen credit, sabotage

2. Effective Self-Promotion
   - Doing enough promoting and socializing of your ideas and results
   - Impactful participation in meetings

3. Executive Presence
   - Have you ever received feedback about your presence and impact?
   - Are you aware of any things you do or don't do that might detract from your presence and impact?
4. Healthy Selfishness
   - Are you overcommitted?
   - Are you able to say no and set boundaries?
   - Are you doing enough self-care?

The 12 Rules you are now going to read about are designed to retain women's advantages and values while guarding against their vulnerabilities.

The Time Factor

Some of you may be wondering about the irony of us suggesting that you start practicing the 12 Rules right after we pointed out that some of you might already be overcommitted. So before we explore the 12 Rules, let's look at the time factor.

In fact, among all the women we have taught the 12 Rules, through coaching and seminars, no one has raised time as a concern. Here's why.

You are already committed to an activity. If you are at a meeting, conference, or on a call, your time is a "sunk cost"; you have to be there. Now, you can hurt yourself (for example, by under-participating, reinforcing negative perceptions, or allowing yourself to be marginalized), or you can apply many of the 12 Rules (such as studying power, detecting deception, managing your "buzz," promoting yourself and your ideas, demonstrating strategic thinking, and improving your executive presence and impact). But it is not a time issue.

Many of the 12 Rules actually free up more of your workweek. By learning how to say no, set boundaries, unwind commitments, and remove yourself from unproductive meetings, you can easily be rewarded with 10 extra hours a week.

Several of the 12 Rules can be combined with other activities. For example, walking and strategic thinking, exercising and networking, and walking meetings.

Finally, we point to a sign sometimes seen at the dentist's office: "You don't have to floss all your teeth, just the ones you want to keep." This is a reminder that we are talking about your career trajectory. Leveraging the 12 Rules stacks the odds in favor of reaching your full potential.

CHAPTER 4

Rule 1:
Study Power

I first started teaching these concepts and skills to women's groups in 1998. The initial program was for an organization founded by Jean Otte called Women Unlimited. It was scheduled for 9:00 a.m. to 5:00 p.m. at the Williams Club on Thirty-Ninth Street in Manhattan. By 10:00 a.m. I thought I was going to be out on that street. There was a mini rebellion to my message, with most of the women saying I was too cynical and negative. One woman stood up for me, and what she said convinced the other women to keep an open mind to my approach. She was a sixty-year-old African American executive at DuPont. She said, "Marty is trying to teach you about power. When I was 10 years old, growing up in the South, I had to study power to survive and to not put my family in harm's way."

If the Power With approach fits your skills and values, I'm not suggesting that you change your leadership style. I am strongly recommending that you also become an expert in power in general, and how power works in your specific organization. Why? This knowledge will enable you to:

- broaden your influence and impact
- get your best ideas implemented
- receive recognition for your contributions
- protect yourself from sabotage
- know when it's time to leave your organization

So let's take the blinders off, go beyond the speeches, vision statements, and core values printed on laminated cards, and learn how to zero in on *reality*. Before we can use our skills and strategies, we need to see clearly how power is used and decisions are made. So if you want to be a quick study on power, here is a checklist of what to focus on.

Shared—or Concentrated—Power

When Sanford Weill took over Citigroup, despite its vast operations and holdings, power was concentrated with him. Soon after he assumed leadership, a common reference was to "friends of Sandy." People loyal and known to him had the access, influence, and the inside track to top positions.

In contrast, Wayne Calloway, CEO of PepsiCo in the eighties, shared power broadly. There were many strong, visible leaders in the business segments and functions like human resources.

In shared power scenarios, there are many possibilities for networking and many paths to success. When power is concentrated, identifying the inner circle and understanding the "scorecard" and priorities become even more important.

Leadership Scorecard and Priorities

The idea of "scorecard" is so important that Rule 6 is dedicated solely to this subject. But I also want to discuss it as part of studying power.

Larry Bossidy, twice voted "toughest CEO," highly valued the ability to execute. In fact, his best-selling book was titled *Execution*.

Indra Nooyi, CEO of PepsiCo—while of course valuing leaders who executed well—often said in speeches that "strategic acuity" was a leadership quality she looked for.

Once you have identified who has power in your organization, the next step is to identify what they look for most in leaders.

It's important to examine who gets promoted, especially when there is a choice between people with different attributes.

We also need to go beyond words and look at actions. For example, you may be encouraged to hear a leader talk about how diversity, equity, and inclusion (DEI) is a top priority. But you also need to track whether anyone has been promoted because they excelled at DEI. Has anyone been demoted because they made no progress in this area?

In short, does the video match the audio?

I know that might sound cynical to some. I prefer to call it realistic. In any case, pursue progress in the area of DEI, but know you will need to score high on other aspects of the scorecard to move your career forward.

It's also important to stay current with the priorities of people in power. Is it margins, market share, collaboration, innovation, cost cutting, customer service? Understanding what is top of mind at the "top of the house" can guide you to the best use of your time, how to add value, and how to get positive attention.

Paula's CEO Perspective

"I work. I have a home. I don't have time to stay current on the priorities of people in power." Sound familiar? We women are so busy, so resolute and committed to our responsibilities that what we do literally is put our head down and work, work, work.

Listen to the airwaves? *"Naaahhh. I don't have time for gossip."* Have a big presentation and stop to ask someone that knows the leaders for feedback? *"Naaah, my work will shine."* Go to the leader directly for pre-guidance? *"Naaah, I will get it right first time around."* Wrong. You don't get it.

Marty had to clearly spell this out to me over several rounds of coaching before I finally understood. I was missing out on the full picture! I had absolutely no idea what the airwaves were saying. I had the habit of repeating the same phrase over again: *"I am the last person in the company to get to know the gossip."* And I said this with pride! How telling this statement was—and how wrong I was. Doing only your job and nothing other than your job is wrong. If you want to be even more effective and competent that you are now, you must do your job *and* listen carefully to the airwaves that speak the true priorities of an organization. As surprising as this may sound, listening to the airwaves makes you stand out much more. It makes you more effective. You start humming on the same wavelength as the leaders.

Taboos

When anthropologists study cultural norms and values, they invariably also discover a culture's taboos. A taboo is a behavior that is harshly discouraged, and someone who breaks a taboo may be shunned or removed from the group.

Every leader grows up with cultural, religious, or family values that shape their personality. Be an anthropologist in your organization and learn about the taboos as early as possible. Sage advice is, "It's healthier to find out where the land mines are by someone pointing them out than by stepping on them."

Not everyone does this, even when the information is readily available. In one company, for example, there were many open jokes about the CEO's attitude toward money.

"He has the first dollar he earned."

"Money goes through his fingers like cement."

"He throws quarters around like manhole covers."

Despite knowing that overspending was a taboo for the CEO, a division leader held a team retreat at a ski resort. He left the organization two months later.

Access and Influence

People in power are often extremely busy and the number of people who get access to them is limited. So it's important to learn:

Who is part of the "inner circle"?

Who gets frequent access to and time with key leaders?

Who has influence and impact on decisions?

Sometimes the answers are not obvious by looking at the org chart. I've seen many situations where an external consulting group or an executive coach or a mentor can exert outside influence. If you are paying attention, being curious, and listening to anecdotes and stories from your network, you will be able to create this access/influence map. While you may not be able to get direct access to top leaders, this knowledge can guide you in developing allies and colleagues who can share information with the "inner circle."

Relative Power

When you attend meetings (whether in person, on the phone, or virtually) or conferences, you can deploy some of the techniques of top poker players.

Poker is a game of information. Top players will gather more information in an hour than an average player gets in a two-day session. They do this by studying "tells," nonverbal behaviors, micro facial or body movements, vocal patterns, deviations from a person's normal habits, and other cues. When you are in any type of group setting, observe carefully how people treat each other. You'll see many signs and signals of people's standing in terms of relative power. For example:

Who does the interrupting and who gets interrupted?

Is there healthy debate, or do people seem hesitant to give their opinion?

Who gets teased?

Whose comments get praised? Who is deferential?

Whose comments get dismissed? If there is conflict, who wins?

Who gets more time?

Whose time gets squeezed or eliminated?

Also, watch body language: touching, standing closer, smiling, and laughing at jokes indicate comfort with another person. At times you will notice stern, dismissive facial expressions and body language. When are leaders surprised, delighted, bored, or angry?

Remember Lois Frankel's research (page 14) on emotional intelligence. You probably score pretty high. Use your scorecard IQ to boost your knowledge about relative power, who is on the inside, who is on the outside, and what leaders are interested in—or bored with. Meetings provide a rich vein of information about power. You probably have to be at the meeting anyway, so you might as well learn all you can.

Power Dynamics: Notice Shifts in Power

In 2010 I was leading a seminar at DIRECTV on the subject of power dynamics. The group consisted of 30 high-potential leaders, and I asked them a question: "Last year, Mike White became your CEO, and three months ago, in July, power shifted dramatically at DIRECTV. Can anyone tell me how the power dynamics have changed and what the implications are for this group?" To give you the context, before Mike joined DIRECTV, human resources was led by someone from the company's treasury department. HR had no power or influence. No one at DTV would have been afraid of HR. No one would have sought their input on key decisions, even people decisions. Mike White was known as an HR-friendly CEO. Sure enough, in July he brought in Joe Bosch, an experienced HR professional (future member of the HR Hall of Fame). Within a short time, if someone had been paying attention, they would have noticed the following:

- Joe was given a position, meeting with the DTV board on certain issues where even Mike was not present.
- Mike started spending more time with Joe than anyone else on his team.
- Mike delegated many people processes (e.g., talent review) and decisions to Joe.
- Joe added a lot of outside talent to his HR team.

In other words, Joe had quickly become the second most powerful person at DTV. And yet, when I asked this question to the group, with Joe actually sitting in the back of the room, no one could provide the right answer. Yet this shift had profound implications for their careers.

The folks at DIRECTV, not noticing this power shift, are not unique. But let's learn from them. Notice the power dynamics in your organization. Stay current with reality.

Power Over/Power With

I'm not going to repeat our discussion of Power With versus Power Over but will just remind you that this is also part of studying power. The quicker we recognize what type of leaders we are dealing with, the better our chances of navigating our circumstances successfully.

Paula's CEO Perspective

I became an intentional observer of leaders and power dynamics. I particularly used Marty's rules above. I looked for "tells," or clues. And very surprisingly, I discovered I was actually pretty good at it. My problem was I wasn't practicing enough. But I could do it. At the end of the day, women are genetically equipped to read tells. The baby is crying? We know why. No language involved. So, I practiced more and more.

Leader 1: Had an on-time obsession. He was always glancing at the agenda and his watch. He had a very time-conscious assistant who managed his agenda with precision. What did I do? When I spoke to him, I started by mentioning how long my presentation would be. I timed myself for presentations. I was brief in my comments. I made tons of references to time: last month, in Quarter 1, same time last year.

Leader 2: Enjoyed humor. He had a relaxed and lighthearted attitude even in the most complex situations. What did I do? I started with a funny story or anecdote when I spoke to him. I used cartoons (that made sense) as first slide in presentations. I inserted humorous comments in the middle of my presentation.

Leader 3: Relationship-based individual. Getting to know you was vital for this chap. What did I do? I invited him for lunch. (This alone was a game-changing occasion in my relationship with this leader. One lunch made a huge difference!) I looked for opportunities for informal talk during the mornings or afternoons. I kept him updated not only on business priorities but also about team-member changes, family issues, and so on. I made sure he knew the people side of our team.

Soon I had a catalog of "leader spins" on every single leader in the organization. It didn't take that long. The massive change was that I did have to develop self-awareness and pay purposeful attention. I was thoughtful about how I was going to pose things to every leader. I flexed accordingly and purposefully. The result was that my job became much easier. My influence increased. My impact in the organization grew to new heights. I became a better leader, completely tuned into what every person needed.

As you can see, we need to become astute about several aspects of power. How much extra time will this take? Two responses: One is that if you keep this top of mind and stay alert and curious, you can gather much of this information from your daily networking, discussions, and meetings. Two, it may take some additional time to think through scenarios, agendas, and the implications of certain decisions.

Maria Nalywayko

Maria is the Chief Human Resource Officer at Sabra Dipping Company, LLC who has served as the top HR leader in premiere companies like T. Rowe Price and CoreLogic. She is known for her intelligence, organizational savvy, strategic business acumen, and work ethic. These qualities all combine to make her a trusted advisor to her CEO partners.

In creating the yearlong Women in Leadership (WIL) program at CoreLogic, Maria has been a pioneer in furthering the advancement and retention of female leaders. The first 12 Rules seminar was launched as part of WIL.

Maria's parents emigrated to the US from Argentina. Like many immigrant families, hers emphasized core values of education, work ethic, and self-reliance, and the belief in "meritocracy." These values and beliefs served her well through education at the US's most prestigious universities, advanced degrees, and her career, which got off to a strong, fast start.

However, around age 30, Maria had a shift in perspective; she started seeing that corporate life was not a pure meritocracy. She was encountering situations where the most deserving people were not always recognized and the best ideas not always supported. Maria decided that to be truly effective in her role and to go as far as she deserved in her career, she needed to become astute about power. She focused on two areas that combined to give her the expertise she needed.

Formal study of power. Going beyond McClelland's Power Over/ Power With model, she studied all aspects of his work on different types of power.

Informal study of power. Just as a poker player looks for tells that reveal information, Maria made a study of the tells of power, which provided a map to show:

- Where the real power was in an organization
- What the unspoken rules were
- What the discrepancies between what was agreed upon at meetings and what actually was done
- What could be changed and what couldn't

Maria credits this combined knowledge about power with enabling her, at different times in her career, to be able to:

- Pivot quickly (i.e., notice change and the implications of change and see it coming)
- Navigate effectively working with multiple leaders who have different orientations to power
- Protect her team's and organization's reputations
- Get her best ideas implemented
- Know when to leave an organization

◆

Rule 1 Self-Assessment

Assess how well you study power. Score yourself in these five areas, with 1 being "not at all," and 5 being "all the time."

1. I pay attention to the signs of Power With or Power Over leadership styles.

   (1)   (2)   (3)   (4)   (5)

2. I determine who has official and unofficial power in my organization.

   (1)   (2)   (3)   (4)   (5)

3. I'm aware of who has access to and influence on power, and in particular who is in "the inner circle."

   (1)   (2)   (3)   (4)   (5)

4. I understand the leadership "scorecard," and the top priorities and taboos of people in power.

   (1)   (2)   (3)   (4)   (5)

5. In meetings I pay attention to the signs and signals of relative power.

   (1)   (2)   (3)   (4)   (5)

Study Power Action Plans

Use your low scores to guide you toward an action plan.

1. ....

....

2. ....

....

3. ....

....

CHAPTER 5

Rule 2:
Detect to Protect

When someone shows you who they are, believe them the first time.
—Maya Angelou

D r. Maya Angelou gave us some essential wisdom for protecting ourselves in our personal and professional lives. Don't fight a war with reality! Rule 2 encourages you to use your emotional intelligence abilities, your "social" IQ, to observe speech and behavior patterns and know quickly whom you are dealing with. We want to be able to see who people are and move beyond how we think they should be.

The discussion we are about to have will be unpleasant for some readers and even uncomfortable for other readers. Here's why:

1. We are going to focus on some positive human traits, like trust, acceptance, forgiveness, and generosity, that if applied to the wrong people can lead to potential career risks.

2. We will be discussing four types of people (high need for control, high need for dominance, overly political, and narcissistic) who are most likely to block your agenda or your career progress. Most of us wish we could avoid dealing with these people entirely. If this person were your brother-in-law who you see once a year, or a neighbor you can ignore, yes, it's possible. But a fact of organizational life is we often have to deal with people we don't like, and don't trust, on a regular basis.

3. I can't write this without sounding alarmist, but my experience coaching thousands of people, and tracking their careers, has shown me that not identifying and not dealing effectively with even one of these types of people can cause a lot of damage.

36

What I'm inviting you to do is to detect patterns of behavior. I'll be giving you several lists of actions to look for. If I see a person exhibiting one of these behaviors, my "antennae" go up and I'll become even more observant. When I see repeated behavior—a pattern—I'm going to take it very seriously. That's because we are all creatures of habit.

To quickly demonstrate the power of habit, I invite you to put down this book for a moment and fold your arms across your body in the most comfortable way. Easy, right? You likely didn't even have to think about it. Now try it again, but put the opposite arm on top as you cross your arms. For most of us this second attempt is quite different. We don't have a habit of folding our arms that way. We have thousands of other habits and patterns that are quick, comfortable, and automatic. Many of them we aren't even aware of until someone else points them out. (Would you have mentioned how you cross your arms on a list of your habits?) You already know that habits and patterns are hard to break, even when you are aware of them and motivated to change. So that is why I am recommending that you take the patterns you observe seriously. The people demonstrating these behaviors would have a hard time changing, even if they were motivated to, and most of them have no desire to change.

As we discuss these types of people, some memories from your past may get triggered. Unless you have led an amazingly charmed life, you may have had encounters that you didn't handle as well as you would have liked or, even worse, left some scars. So I invite you to read and reflect. In particular, consider if there were situations where you were too:

Naive *"I would never do that to him. Why would he do that to me?"*

Trusting *"He said it was unintentional. He just forgot to give me the information in time."*

Rationalizing *"He has a lot of other wonderful qualities."*

Forgiving *"She apologized and said it wouldn't happen again."*

If in the past you were burned because you missed or dismissed some signals, in a real sense you have already paid for the lesson. So we might as well extract the learning. When it comes to trusting others, I've heard a variety of approaches:

"I trust people until they prove me wrong."

"I like to give people the benefit of the doubt."

"I assume positive intent."

Maybe it's because I grew up in Brooklyn, New York, but I prefer a more earned trust model. (At the candy store on my street corner, there was a big sign: "In God we trust; everyone else pays cash.") This model is called *Working Trust*.

The Working Trust starting point is that I am going to trust people enough so that we can engage, share, and work together; then I can keenly observe their behavior. If they do what they say they are going to do, meet their commitments, keep information confidential, and so on, I move them more solidly into the Zone of Trust. If I start to see some patterns that we are about to discuss, I will shift to more protective strategies.

What to Look For

High Need for Control

Definition: *The degree to which someone has a strong desire for control of decision-making and the resources necessary to achieve desired outcomes.*

Need for Control	2 Points Generally True	1 Point Somewhat True	0 Points Rarely True
1. Having control over your surroundings gives you a sense of security and safety			
2. You like situations where you know that you have the resources and skills to achieve a result and are minimally dependent on the actions of others			
3. It is very important to you to have clarity about roles, responsibilities, and decision-making authority			
4. You strongly prefer roles where you are the decision maker and may get frustrated in a heavily matrixed, consensus driven organization			
5. When power or leadership authority are not clearly defined, you move easily into a decision-making role			

Total: _____ point(s)

People who score 8 to 10 on this scale are very common in organizations. The main reason to recognize their high need for control is to anticipate the challenges they have working in a shared-power structure. A matrix, cross-functional team or any shared decision-making process with them often will surface "turf" issues over controlling information and conflicts about decision-making rights.

High Need for Dominance

Definition: *The extent to which someone has a strong desire for power over others and difficulty establishing 50-50 relationships.*

Need for Dominance	2 Points Generally True	1 Point Somewhat True	0 Points Rarely True
1. Having power over other people gives you a feeling of security and safety			
2. You enjoy the feeling that people are somewhat afraid of you			
3. You expect people to be deferential to you			
4. When you are not in a dominant role you may feel weak and vulnerable			
5. You tend to evaluate people in terms of how much power they have			

Someone scoring 8 to 10 on this scale, especially if they also have a high need for control, is going to present quite a few difficulties for a Power With leader. For now, my goal is for you to see how this person is wired.

- They see relationships in terms of power differences.
- If they are not "top dog," they experience stress and vulnerability.
- They enjoy intimidating others.
- They often interpret politeness, kindness as "weakness."

Overly Political: Behaviors to be Aware of

- Exaggerations
- Overpromising
- Taking undeserved credit

- Hiding bad news
- Giving only partial information
- Lying
- Insincere flattery
- Unfairly tarnishing reputations
- Superficial explanations
- Guarded/evasive speech
- Not admitting mistakes, blaming others, or making excuses
- Deferential to people in power; dismissive or disrespectful to people with less power
- Giving differing versions of events to different people
- Not eliminating conflicts of interest
- Punishing people who challenge or disagree
- Overly controlling of information

These people are defined by two negative qualities.

- They put their self-interest above the interests of the organizations' shareholders, customers, and clients (and certainly above yours).
- They will do what they can get away with, i.e., if they can take credit for your work, blame someone else for their mistakes, hide or distort information, or take more than their share of resources with no consequences, they will.

Of course, OPs don't wear signs revealing who they are. In fact, their statements (*"There are no politics in my organization." "This may hurt me personally, but it's the right thing for the organization."*) often say the opposite.

So although we can't always put our full faith in people's words, we can give a lot of credence to their behavior. By definition OPs are trying to hide their personal or hidden agendas. When you observe these patterns of behavior or your network gives you a warning about someone, take it seriously.

Shift into a protective mode to guard your reputation, resources, and ideas. This often involves documenting discussions and agreements, leveraging your network, and deploying several of the other 12 Rules.

Narcissistic Behaviors

Narcissists might make up only a small percentage of the overall population (1 to 3 percent), but they have some characteristics that unfortunately allow them to survive and even thrive in organizational life, including relentless self-promotion and exaggerating their contributions; the ability to convincingly deceive others because they believe their own lies; and putting on "charm offensives" long enough to use people for their own needs. Other traits of narcissism include:

- a need for admiration, attention
- a lack of empathy
- a need for special treatment
- a sense of grandiosity or belief in their superiority
- a lack of tolerance for criticism ("narcissistic wound")
- a pattern of taking advantage of others without remorse
- a tendency to "gaslight" others

One of the most toxic, potentially crazy-making aspects of a narcissist is their ability to gaslight someone. The term comes from a 1944 movie, *Gaslight*, starring Charles Boyer as a husband who attempts to undermine his wife's (Ingrid Bergman) confidence and ultimately her sanity. Narcissists do this by rewriting history, insisting they never said things, challenging your recollections, blaming you for their mistakes, and accusing you of possessing negative traits that they in fact have.

When someone attempts to gaslight you, they are trying to take away your power by undermining your confidence or even your sense of reality.

It's extremely important to see this behavior for what it is or, even better, stop it cold. In 2020, Nikki Haley, then US ambassador to the UN, demonstrated this vividly. At one point she weighed in on an issue facing the administration, differing from several members of the cabinet. One cabinet member got in front of the cameras and said, "I think Ambassador Haley was confused." Within minutes Haley spoke to the press and firmly said, "I don't get confused." She understood she was being gaslighted and not only countered that attempt but probably stopped others from trying it in the future.

Two other concepts to keep in mind when dealing with narcissists:

Narcissistic Supply: Since the narcissist needs a steady supply of attention, recognition, flattery, and agreement, you will always find people on the team who are providing this "supply." Loyalty is valued more highly than competence. That is why narcissists are never as smart, funny, or attractive as the people around them are saying.

Narcissistic Wound: Criticism or even implied criticism is devastating to a narcissist and is known as a "wound." They often lash out at or exclude people who give them corrective feedback. This is one of many reasons why being with a narcissist requires increased vigilance and is so draining.

The verbal skills you will learn in several of the rules, as well as your ability to say no and maintain boundaries, will help you cut your losses with narcissists. But the best advice, either in your professional or personal life, is to minimize your interactions with them.

Paula's CEO Perspective

A long time ago I had a narcissistic boss. The first time Marty mentioned this concept to me I was dumbfounded. *"A narcissistic boss! Is that even possible?"* I wondered. After he explained further, I did what we thorough women always do: I researched. To my surprise, I found extensive science about narcissistic personalities in the workplace. I still hold on to a file where I copy-pasted everything I could find on the issue. I reread, analyzed, and concluded: Marty is darn right. I do have a narcissistic boss. He fits the profile 100 percent. That is when you become smarter and you find a way to work around the constant tension.

I changed and adapted. I invented a few rules that came in handy.

Rule 1. When we spoke, I always started by congratulating him about something.

"Hi! I really liked your intervention in X meeting last week! You made us all think!"

"Good morning! I am so grateful you caught the complicated issue on time."

"Hello, you were nothing short than spectacular as you addressed the board. I told everyone how brilliant you were."

And guess what? He ate it up.

Even if we were on the phone, I could tell how pleased he was that I was outspoken about his brilliant contributions.

Rule 2. During our conversations, I made sure he understood I was "copying" him and that I recognized how genius his ideas were.

"Ohhhhh! I see your point perfectly. It is such a great idea!"

"How come nobody ever thought about that before?"

Rule 3. I ended every conversation with praise, just as I had started.

"So happy we could connect. Your help was incredible."

"This call was very worthwhile. You have given us something to think about."

I know what you are thinking: *This is so Machiavellian. I could never do this.* You are wrong. I was still doing my job and results were incredibly solid. I was still communicating to upper management what needed to be communicated. The only thing that had changed was my personal awareness of leadership styles and my ability to adapt to that style in a manner that allowed me to do my job even better. The tension in our calls disappeared. I could feel him melting with my praise. After that, I went straight to the point and was super professional about whatever business needed to be done. Slight changes in communication made my life easier, my boss happier, and business more fluid. No damage was done.

Personal Life

Our colleague Hila Angel works on projects that focus on violence against women, and most importantly develop methods for women to defend themselves. She notes that most violent incidents against women are instigated by romantic partners or occur during dating. So in addition to the career incentives to pay attention to the behavior patterns described in Rule 2 (need for control, need to dominate, deception, narcissism) she believes these warning signals can also alert you to risks in your personal life. As George Orwell noted, " If you want to know who rules over you, look at who you are not allowed to criticize."

Trustworthy Behaviors

In addition to discovering who *not* to trust, it's also important for our emotional well-being and effectiveness to identify allies we *can* trust. So we want to notice when people:

- Do what they say they are going to do
- Meet their deadlines and commitments
- Keep information confidential
- Give you feedback in a respectful, helpful way
- Are consistent about giving others the credit they deserve
- Admit the mistakes and accept responsibility for their actions
- Share information in a timely, open manner
- Check things out with you before jumping to conclusions

By embracing Rule 2 you will know who you are dealing with and be better able to predict their actions. You will start to see it coming, and Rules 3 to 12 will equip you with skills and strategies to protect yourself and maintain a positive career trajectory.

Paula's CEO Perspective

Am I a Power With CEO? Does it hurt me? I am sure it has. More than once. It takes time to, and a significant amount of personal awareness to feel comfortable using your power. Here is a story by way of example. I live and work in Mexico, a place where, as you might imagine, hierarchy is particularly important. Sometimes I would arrive late to a meeting and quietly go sit at the back trying to make myself invisible, worried I was interrupting the flow of the conversation, and ashamed of being late. Then the same exact scenario would happen. Someone, usually a male colleague, would stand up and give me his chair. Usually at a dominant place at the table. At the beginning I was super embarrassed about taking the seat. *"No, no, no! That's OK. I will sit in the back."* Finally, it dawned at me.

I just had to take the power seat I was being offered! It belonged to me. And it is seated at the helm or in that power seat that I can maximize my positive influence on the team and business. But it took me a long time to understand that, for others, the hierarchal seat was more important than for me. I could not care less where I am seated, what size my office is, or what car I drive. However, for many others, these are power symbols that make a difference. Look for those power symbols and use them! Do not shy away from them like I did. You are there to use them to elevate your positive influence.

◆

Rule 2 Self-Assessment

Assess how well you Detect to Protect. Score yourself in these five areas, with 1 being "not at all," and 5 being "all the time."

1. I notice the behaviors of high-need-for-control individuals, and I have skills to be effective with them.

   ① ② ③ ④ ⑤

2. I can anticipate and predict the actions of high-need-to-dominate individuals.

   ① ② ③ ④ ⑤

3. I know who the overly political people are in my organization.

   ① ② ③ ④ ⑤

4. I minimize the interactions I have with narcissists and can protect myself from gaslighting.

   ① ② ③ ④ ⑤

5. I know whom to trust and whom not to trust.

① ② ③ ④ ⑤

Detect to Protect Action Plans

Use your low scores to guide you toward an action plan.

1. ....

....

2. ....

....

3. ....

....

CHAPTER 6

Rule 3A: Use Your Power

Rule 3B: Don't Give Away Your Power

Soon after Nancy Pelosi was selected as Speaker of the US House of Representatives, she was interviewed on TV in front of a live audience of women. Asked for her advice to aspiring female leaders, she replied, "Know your power." Weeks later she made history by forcing President Trump to postpone his yearly State of the Union address. The Constitution says that the Speaker of the House has the right to invite the president to make that speech to a joint session of Congress. Speaker Pelosi knew her power and used it to dramatic effect.

Rule 3A: Use Your Power

If everyone were as comfortable using power as Nancy Pelosi is, I wouldn't bother with giving you Rule 3. Unfortunately, I've encountered many situations where leaders were ambivalent, tentative, or too slow to use their power.

I'm going to share one of these examples. I selected a case study involving Anne (not her real name) because Anne is one of the highest-level female CEOs in the world. My goal is for you to see that even she had some blind spots about using power. What happened to her also illustrates examples of why Rules 1 and 2 are so important. Please read Anne's story and take a little time to reflect on some questions provided.

Charles is the president of the snack division of a large food and beverage multinational company. Recently he was thrilled to learn that the board had selected him to replace the current CEO when he retired in three months. The chairman of the board explained to Charles that this would give him time to find his replacement at the snack division. Charles replied that he already had a good choice for that role, Stuart R, the current head of sales. The chairman pushed back, saying, "We don't think Stuart is ready, and we prefer you look outside the company. Please evaluate all strong female candidates."

After an accelerated search process, Charles was able to convince Anne, the CEO of a smaller competitor, to lead the snack division. He explained that he expected to be CEO for five years and hoped that she would be able to replace him and become the company's first female CEO. With regards to Stuart, he told Anne that it was "her call" whether to keep Stuart in her division or send him to work in another business unit. He expressed that his preference would be for her to retain and mentor him so that he could be her backup. She replied that she looked forward to working with him and also learning from him.

In the snack division, Anne renewed her relationship with Francoise, a VP of human resources, who had worked with Anne twelve years earlier. When they went out to lunch, Francoise took a deep breath and said, "Anne, I am taking a big risk in telling you this, but we go back a long way and I want to give you a heads-up about the situation you are walking into. If you use this information, please don't say you heard it from me."

She went on to explain that Charles and Stuart were extremely close. They had not only worked together for 15 years but had very strong religious and geographical ties.

To make things worse, she explained, Stuart benefited from the "halo effect" and could do no wrong in Charles's opinion. In the past Stuart had used his close relationship and frequent communication with Charles to blame (bad-mouth) and marginalize his rivals in the company. Francoise concluded by strongly recommending that Anne "ship" Stuart to another division while she was in the "honeymoon" period with the power to do so.

Anne thanked Francoise for the information and advice but expressed that she was not worried about Stuart, saying, "I am in a very strong position. Charles needs me and Stuart needs me to mentor him to replace me some day."

Over the next three months the following events occurred:

- Stuart neglected to invite Anne to some key meetings. When she learned about it, he explained that he did not think the meetings were the best use of her time and that Charles did not attend those meetings when he was in her role.
- On several occasions Stuart withheld key information from Anne. Twice, when Charles asked her questions related to these matters, she was unable to answer.
- Stuart arranged to have weekly calls with Charles, without Anne's knowledge. When Charles would ask about how Anne was doing, Stuart would use phrases like "She doesn't seem to like getting her hands dirty," "I think she likes to operate at 30,000 feet," and "She's great at the macro but doesn't seem interested in learning about the micro." Stuart's comments were sure to alarm and upset Charles, who liked hands-on leaders who were knowledgeable about the details of their business.

Case Study Questions and Analysis

- What mistakes did Anne make?
- Why do you think Anne didn't pay more attention to the warning about Stuart and use her power to protect herself?
- What should Anne do now?

In life it's much less costly to learn from other people's mistakes, so I want to highlight some key takeaways from this case study.

1. **Not taking Francoise's warning very seriously.**
   When someone comes to you to warn you about a threat, when not only is there nothing in it for them but they take a personal risk by informing you, at the minimum it should prompt you to be a vigilant observer. If Anne had done this, she would have noticed much sooner how Stuart was marginalizing her regarding meetings and withholding information.

2. **Ignoring Rule 2: Detect to Protect.**
   Francoise described behavior patterns and tactics often deployed by overly political people. These actions had worked for Stuart in the past. He would be extremely unlikely to change.

3. **Not focusing on Charles's scorecard.**

Stuart knew exactly how to create a negative perception of Anne. Charles expected hands-on leaders familiar with the details of their business. Comments about "30,000 feet" and macro versus micro go directly against Charles's scorecard and raise concerns about Anne's leadership.

Why didn't Anne use her power? I eventually coached Anne, and what I learned was that two things led her to hesitate to "ship" Stuart to another division:

- She was too unselfish for the situation. She thought of Charles's and Stuart's needs instead of putting her needs and her self-protection first.
- She had a false sense of comfort. She prided herself on her ability to collaborate, persuade, and win people over. This prevented her from seeing that this actually encourages someone like Stuart to continue marginalization and sabotage.

What should Anne do now?

Anne was able to recover from her missteps. She became a student of power (Rule 1) and became very knowledgeable about Charles's scorecard. She immersed herself in the details of the business and prepared well for the type of questions Charles asked. She explained to Charles that her transition with Stuart was complete and that for his continued growth as a leader he needed to work in another division of the company. She pointed to the fact that he had spent his entire career in one business. Charles agreed and Stuart left a month later. So let's learn from Anne. Study power. Detect to protect. Use your power.

Rule 3B: Don't Give Away Your Power

There are many ways that people give away their power. We are going to examine three of them in this book: allowing yourself to be marginalized (see Rule 10, pages 114-120), allowing others to "trigger" unhelpful emotions (see Rule 11, pages 121-137), and having a high need for approval.

High Need for Approval

Care about what others think and you will always be their prisoner. —Lao-tzu

Twenty-five hundred years ago, Lao-tzu wandered through China mostly alone. I doubt he was ever part of any organization. So his comment concerning caring about what others think is too extreme for most of us. We do need to be concerned with, to a certain extent, how others are regarding us. But I wanted to start our discussion with his quote because it contains a penetrating insight about the need for approval. If our need for approval is too high, we will routinely give other people power over our moods, energy, presence, and confidence. So let's define this need for approval and break it down to specific behaviors.

Need For Approval

Definition: *This indicates the degree to which your self-image and self-satisfaction are dependent on the good opinions and approval of others.*

Need for Approval	2 Points Generally True	1 Point Somewhat True	0 Points Rarely True
1. It is very important to you that other people like you			
2. You make an extra effort to find out what other people are looking for and try to give them what they want			
3. In order to ensure harmonious relationships, you spend a lot of time building alignment and consensus and looking for a win–win			
4. To maintain smooth relationships you find yourself suppressing criticism, overaccommodating, or acquiescing			
5. You sometimes discover that you have interpreted someone's behavior toward you as disapproving, when in fact that was not the case			

Please score yourself on each of the items. If your total is in the 7 to 10 range, the odds are your need for approval is hurting you in a variety of ways. For example:

- Your moods and energy levels will too often shift based on other people's facial expressions, body language, comments, or lack of response to you.
- Rather than operating from a centered, confident stance, you will feel more anxious because your well-being is in the hands of others, which detracts from your executive presence.

- More often than is good for you, you may suppress your needs, or ideas, or critical feedback.

- You may acquiesce or say yes to requests, leaving you overcommitted.

My recommendation is that over time you work to reduce your need for approval down to the 4 to 6 range. Here is how to do it:

- **Be selective.** Let's concede that a small group of people do need to support and approve of you so you can achieve your goals. But we don't want to reduce our power and presence by wanting everyone's approval. So narrow down the "need to" list. Other people you deal with can be in a "nice to" category, that is, you would like their approval, but you are not going to be upset if you don't get it.

- **Really internalize what too high a need for approval is costing you.** Reread the list of consequences. Commit yourself to retaining your center, your inner control over your power.

- **Determine what is "normal" for another person.** I have a friend who was continually frustrated with her boss's lack of warmth and recognition. I pointed out that this was normal for her boss. He treated everyone like that, so my friend was giving away her power by taking this behavior personally and continuing to expect something she was unlikely to get. So, if you work with someone who routinely withholds smiles, recognition, and validation, please recalibrate your expectations. You will be a lot happier.

- **Don't jump to conclusions.** Guess what? Many, many times when other people aren't smiling at us, don't acknowledge our greeting, don't react to our ideas with the enthusiasm we want, or don't respond to our emails or voice mails, *it has nothing to do with us.* They are busy with other things, they didn't read or get the message, they are distracted with personal concerns, they didn't sleep well, or they missed their favorite breakfast. It could be related to you, but don't assume it is. Be patient and check things out before you torture yourself with negative scenarios.

- **Determine if it is a catastrophe or an inconvenience.** Mark Twain once remarked, "My life has been a series of horrible misfortunes, most of which never happened." So, please challenge yourself in this way. If someone doesn't recognize you or appreciate you the way you would like, ask yourself: Is this an inconvenience, a setback, a disappointment—or is it a "horrible misfortune," a catastrophe? If you remind yourself that, for many of the people you relate to, their lack of approval is more in the inconvenience/disappointment category, you will retain your inner core of power.

Paula's CEO Perspective

I tend to be the opposite of what Marty describes. I have an exceptionally low need for approval. I don't need warmth and recognition. I do get it that people are extremely busy and I don't take things personally. When this is paired with remarkably high standards for everyone and everything, you can have a real issue. It took me time to understand that not everyone was like me and that it was important as a senior business leader to spread out warmth, recognition, and approval to others. Here again I became watchful of my language and sharpened my communication skills. Celebrating the *journey* and the hard work of the team working on complex problem solving became important. In feedback sessions and one-on-ones with managers, I was conscious of bringing up the positive impact of that person first and foremost. It doesn't take long to recognize that a few, correctly placed words of encouragement can go a long way in making individuals content and satisfied with their contributions. Because it wasn't something I needed, I was not using enough positive encouragement. Creating smiles is better business, no doubt.

Calm Self-Critique (CSC)

For a moment please think about a young person who you really care about (your child, a niece or nephew, a friend or family member). You want to pass along to this person something that will help them have a happier, more fulfilled life.

If you could pick only one of the following for this person, what would it be?

- Lots of money
- Access to an Ivy League education

- The skill of a calm self-critique

We would choose calm self-critique. Why? We all know or have read about people who ran through a lot of money or squandered their opportunities at university. Calm self-critique, a skill developed by Dr. Albert Ellis, Ph.D., would allow this person to become a lifelong learner, reduce their stress, and significantly increase their chances of reaching their full potential.

The reason we are describing it here, as part of a plan to reduce a high need for approval, is that CSC can inoculate you against the sting of disapproval and diminish your fear of criticism. There are three components to CSC:

1. **Self-Acceptance.** CSC starts with the acceptance that I'm a fallible human being. I know I have blind spots about my behavior, skill deficits, and knowledge gaps. I know I'm not perfect and don't need to be. As some people like to say, "God is not finished with me yet."

2. **Self-Confidence.** I also know that I can learn and improve. Receiving candid, specific feedback, studying exemplars, or having a teacher or coach guide me can all put me on a path to acquire knowledge and skill or change my behaviors.

3. **Self-Care.** I refuse to call myself names, beat myself up, or become my own worst critic. When I fall short of my standards, make mistakes, or receive disapproval from others, I calmly consider the information and decide how to or *if* I will improve. (Let's come back to this "if" in a moment). A vivid example of how CSC is a part of self-care revolves around how we talk to ourselves when we perform poorly. Probably the only thing some people fear more than speaking to a large audience is giving a speech to that audience that is boring, low impact, and not appreciated.

Unfortunately, that is what happened to me the first time I spoke to an audience of 500 people. At the time, fall 1977, my job was to travel around the US and write material for a very entertaining speaker, Larry Wilson, founder of Wilson Learning. Leading up to a daylong program with Wells Fargo Bank in San Francisco, Larry said to me, "Marty, you helped me create this workshop. Why don't you present part of it?" Up to that point in my career I had only facilitated seminars with a dozen participants. But I said yes. Things did not go well to say the least. The techniques that worked in small groups did not go over well in a group of 500. I knew it wasn't my imagination when I overheard someone at lunch say, "I hope Larry Wilson comes back onstage this afternoon."

Let's take a look at how I could have talked to myself.

> *"Marty, you are an idiot. Why did you ever think you could get on a stage with Larry Wilson? This was embarrassing. You stink at this kind of presentation. Just go back to your small groups and stay there."*

How would this have made me feel? Where is the opportunity for learning and improvement? Nowhere, because I just shut the door.

Henry Ford once remarked, "One person says, 'I can do it,' one person says, 'I can't do it,' and they both turn out to be right."

If I had the skill of CSC, here is how I might have coached myself.

> *"Marty, that was disappointing. I can see there were several things about this setting that I underestimated. If I want to continue to talk to an audience of this size, I am going to need to improve. Having done it this first time, I can spot several things I would do differently. I'm sure Larry could point out many errors of omission and commission. I'm going to ask him for candid, specific feedback. I'll learn from the master."*

Now let's come back to the reason we inserted an "if" in "*if* you will improve." Many times, when you receive negative feedback or the disapproval of others, it says as much about them as it does about you. So it is very helpful to distinguish between *preference feedback* and *performance feedback*. Preference feedback is simply information about how another person wants you to do something, what their standards are, or how they want you to interact with them. Performance feedback relates to skills and behaviors that are important to your objectives or overall effectiveness.

So we suggest when you receive feedback from others:

- Center your body.
- Breathe deeply.
- Listen carefully.
- Ask yourself some questions to discern how you will react to the feedback:

  Have I heard this before?

  Could other people have similar reactions?

  Is this important to my performance or values?

Is this simply information about this person's preferences, what's important to them, or how they want to be treated?

The answers to these questions will guide you to how or *if* you are going to change. The process of calmly, nondefensively listening to and evaluating feedback removes stress and allows you to regain your power.

·· LEADERSHIP PROFILE ··

Marcela del Carmen

Marcela came to the US when she was 10 years old, from Managua, Nicaragua. She was fortunate in that her parents emphasized self-reliance and education for both the boys and girls in the family, and she left for college when she was 17.

Her educational journey took her all the way to the Faculty of Medicine at Harvard University. Marcela was the first woman and first Latina to be elevated to professor of obstetrics, gynecology, and reproductive biology. Her clinical excellence, innovative surgical techniques and procedures, and novel therapies have made her a world-renowned gynecologic oncologist. Over the years she has received recognition from many sources, including the McGovern Award for Clinical Excellence. Marcela's dedication to her patients and joy in being a doctor is such that she often remarks, "I get more from my patients than I can ever give them."

As her career as a clinician progressed, Marcela became concerned about representation levels, career pacing, and pay issues related to women faculty. She decided to shift toward leadership and eventually executive roles, primarily as a way to open doors for others. She became the chief medical officer at Massachusetts General Hospital (MGH) and recently was promoted to be the president of the Physicians Organization, which includes over 3,200 doctors.

As part of her professional development as an executive, Marcela devoted herself to learning and leveraging the 12 Rules. Rule 4 (Buzz), Rule 5 (Scorecard), and even reminders about self-care (Rules 11 and 12) were useful, but it was in reading about Rule 3 that she identified her potential Achilles' heel, a high need for approval. While she had always been aware of this tendency, it was a wake-up call for her to view it through the lens of not giving away her power.

She was leading a group of over 3,000 doctors, many of whom had strong, diverse, and vocal opinions about the direction of the hospital system. At the same time, senior leadership at MGH was moving toward significant changes, including a new structure through integration. Marcela saw that her need for approval could divert her focus, drain her energy, and diminish her decisiveness. With Marcela, it's rarely about her, and she keeps her eyes on the prize, delivering the highest-quality service to MGH's patients, community, and research beneficiaries. Through a series of town halls, she combined the best of her skills and values while keeping Rule 3 top of mind. She listened to everyone and validated their concerns. Where necessary, she provided missing information and pushed back on misguided rumors or misinformation. She didn't get knocked off course when people didn't agree with her or didn't like certain decisions. She was able to discern personal agendas or perspectives that didn't represent the majority of the physicians or the goals of improving patient care and access. The process led many participants to recognize Marcela's selflessness, courage, and willingness to hear diverse opinions and criticism.

As can often happen, when Marcela lowered her need for approval, her personal approval and the recognition of her leadership increased.

◆

Rule 3 Self-Assessment

Use Your Power/Don't Give Away Your Power. Score yourself in these five areas, with 1 being "not at all," and 5 being "all the time."

1. I have an accurate picture of how much power I have.
   1   2   3   4   5

2. I know the power of the allies in my network.
   1   2   3   4   5

3. I am comfortable using the power I have.
   1   2   3   4   5

4. I don't give my power away to others by excessively needing their approval.

①   ②   ③   ④   ⑤

5. I can calmly and clearly consider criticism and corrective feedback.

①   ②   ③   ④   ⑤

Use Your Power/Don't Give Away Your Power Action Plans

Use your low scores to guide you toward an action plan.

1. ....

....

2. ....

....

3. ....

....

CHAPTER 7

Rule 4:
Know Your Buzz

The difference between reality and perception is that people often make decisions based on perception.
—Anonymous

Perception. Many of us don't like that word, especially when it applies to decisions about our career. We want those decisions to be objective and fair, based on our accomplishments and capabilities. The reason I used this quote to start this discussion about knowing your buzz is to remind you that some of these key decision-makers are busy people, prone, just as we are, to being influenced by sound bites and incidents. Their perceptions can be shaped by anecdotes or comments they hear but don't take the time to check out. Your "buzz" is your reputation, what people say when your name comes up. ***Not knowing your buzz puts you at an extreme disadvantage.*** Here are just a few buzz watchouts:

- **Getting pigeonholed.** This means being put in a career box that can be difficult to break out of. Sometimes we have a "success problem" in that we are very good at something and get a reputation that is positive but limiting. *"Subject matter expert," "Katherine is our 'Ms. Fix-it.' She can tackle any problem."* Sometimes we pigeonhole ourselves. If you go into meeting after meeting and use a lot of technical jargon and focus your remarks only on your function, the buzz will be "functional" and you won't be considered for broader roles. If you consistently discuss specific projects in quite a bit of detail, perceptions like "tactical" or "in the weeds" may become part of your buzz.

- **Buzz based on missing information or misinformation.** Remember: you are not in the room when your future is being discussed. If someone at the table doesn't know that you have had P&L responsi-bilities, successfully launched a new product, or managed teams, the organization will not make an informed decision. Similarly, they can make a decision based on wrong information. Natasha went to her manager and expressed surprise and frustration that she wasn't con-sidered for a recent promotion. It was a role she felt fully qualified for. Her manager replied, "You are qualified. But I heard that because of your father-in-law's health, you are not willing to relocate your family at this time." Natasha's frustration only deepened because the reality was that her sister-in-law's family had agreed to care for her father-in-law if Natasha was offered a promotion that required relocation.

- **"Managing the airwaves" to create harmful buzz.** Let's go back to our case study of Anne and Stuart (pages 47-50). Notice that Stu-art used his access to Charles to "manage the airwaves" about Anne. By describing her as operating at "30,000 feet" or "not wanting to get her hands dirty," he leveraged his knowledge of Charles's score-card. Given Charles's approach to leadership, this was very dam-aging buzz. Imagine another scenario where someone is seeking to "get some mud" on me and create negative buzz. We both work in an organization led by a CEO who emphasizes strategic thinking as the essential leadership capability. My adversary uses his access to someone in the CEO's inner circle and offers the "feedback": "That Marty Seldman is a good guy. If you point him in the right direction, you can take it to the bank. Now, you have to call the plays for him, but he's very solid and dependable." If I don't know about this buzz and don't correct it, my future progression in this organization is very much in doubt.

- **Buzz based on reality.** In fact, all of us have skill deficits, knowl-edge gaps, and blind spots about our impact. Sometimes the buzz is telling us we need to be a better listener, run more effective meetings, or think longer term. If you go to meeting after meeting and are too quiet or under-participate based on your knowledge and expertise, your buzz may include "She is a gray spot on a gray wall," and you will have earned it.

Hopefully you are getting motivated to discover your buzz, but I want to summarize three compelling reasons to make this a priority:

1. If you don't know the decision-makers are missing key information,

you won't be able to provide it. If you don't know they are misinformed, you won't be able correct it.

2. If you don't know the negative buzz about yourself, you will likely continue to reinforce those perceptions. You've probably heard the advice, "If you are in a deep hole, the first thing to do is stop digging." The same wisdom applies to buzz. Never reinforce negative buzz!

3. If you don't know your buzz, you won't be able to make a specific, targeted action plan to either change your behavior and/or acquire new skills (if the buzz is based on reality) or take visible steps to change perceptions.

So I hope now you can see that even if the buzz is undeserved, even if you think it's 180 degrees wrong, you always want to know what it is. I can give you hundreds of examples of how not knowing the buzz put women at a disadvantage, but I'm going to share one, precisely because the situation was unfair and at odds with reality. I'm also using this case study because Maria was able to learn her buzz, turn things around, and get the recognition she deserved. As with the previous case study (Anne, pages 47-50), after you have studied it, please answer the reflection questions.

Maria is a vice president of product development in an automotive parts manufacturing company. She is known as a true Power With leader and has been recognized for her skills in collaboration, team building, and coaching individuals on her team.

The company's engagement surveys always indicate that people really enjoy working with her. Maria has a pleasant personal style and is often seen with a ready smile. She believes that she has a responsibility to champion her people, so during talent reviews she focuses on their strengths and potential. If her boss or one of her peers offers critical feedback about someone on her team, she tends to defend that person at the talent review. She does take the feedback about her people seriously but prefers to discuss it with the individual in private.

In general, this fits Maria's approach to leading people. She will have "tough love" conversations with team members when necessary—always privately and confidentially. This also applies when she feels someone's performance or behavior is hurting the team and they need to be changed out. She does so respectfully and privately as opposed to some of her peers, who boast of "public floggings."

Maria doesn't have a high need for attention and doesn't participate as much as her peers at meetings. If she has conflicts with them, she prefers to resolve them in a one-on-one setting.

For the past six quarters, her results have been ahead of plan. These numbers, combined with the fact that the company's vision and values statement emphasizes collaboration and mutual respect, have Maria expecting to be strongly considered for expanded responsibilities. Recently she asked her human resources partner about whether there was support for her promotion when Maria was discussed at talent review. The HR partner replied, "Unfortunately, although people appreciate your contribution and cohesive team, there were significant questions about your toughness and gravitas. They think this industry is populated with quite a few tough males at higher levels, and they are afraid you may be too nice and too polite."

Maria was shocked and extremely upset. "This is BS! These guys talk tough, but they don't give people tough feedback or confront bad behavior. I do. They don't fire people. They move them to other parts of the company. I take people out if they are hurting the company. This is so unfair. I am actually tougher than any of them."

Case Study Questions and Analysis

Do you think the current perception (buzz) about Maria is fair or unfair? What errors of omission and/or commission did Maria make that contributed to this buzz? What steps should Maria take to change how she is perceived?

I became Maria's executive coach. I entered into the assignment expecting the issues would be around "toughness" but discovered that was not Maria's problem. She needed insights about buzz, optics, and how to create accurate perceptions. Reading the case study, you can see that when Maria was appropriately direct and forceful, no one saw it. In public, people saw friendly, polite, supportive behaviors. After understanding the root cause of the buzz, Maria created an action plan that quickly showed senior management that she had the qualities they were looking for.

1. **Smile selectively.** Going forward Maria monitored her smiling. In particular she made sure to have a serious expression when discussing conflicts, or business or personnel issues.

2. **Let people know about her "tough love" discussions and timely calls on people.** "I've spoken to Jim about his behavior. He knows he has 90 days to demonstrate visible improvement, otherwise we are going to have a different kind of discussion."

3. **Make balanced presentations during talent review.** Maria spent more time on her assessment of direct reports developmental needs. She also was more inviting of her peers' constructive feedback about her team.

4. **Be more willing to challenge others publicly.** Maria went to meetings with an increased willingness to respectfully challenge or push back on her peers. She was more often heard using phrases like, "I have a different point of view"; "I'm not as confident as you are that this approach is going to get us where we need to go"; "I've listened carefully and here is my remaining concern. I haven't heard an answer to how we avoid this risk."

Finding Out Your Buzz

So if you are now motivated to discover your buzz, how do you do it? Rick Brandon and I developed a checklist for this in our 2004 book, *Survival of the Savvy.*

Ask Others

Your network can tell you what others are saying about you, your unit, or that new project you're pushing.

- **Colleagues**. Peers know your public image. Ask people you trust to give you the straight scoop without pulling punches. Make sure they're wired in enough themselves to know and that they don't have an ulterior motive for feeding you false information. (Just because you're paranoid doesn't mean people aren't out to get you!)

- **Direct Reports**. Your team may have access to more data than your peers, since others may be less cautious about leveling with them. They may be eager to help out, but make sure they don't tell you what they *think* you want to hear. Reassure them that they won't become messengers who are killed for bearing bad news.

- **Cross-Organizational Contacts**. Tap into people outside of your area. Enlist "murmur mentors" from your contacts at trainings, cross-functional meetings, or corporate functions.

- **Managers**. Use your boss as a confidante, depending upon your relationship and whether she is open and honest. A manager who understands organizational savvy can be asked at lunch in a casual manner. Make sure the boss knows you can handle straight feedback. If your manager is more formal, use sanctioned times such as appraisals. Sometimes, your boss's boss has a broader perspective, but solicit this input only if it's safe, appropriate, and (usually) after you've interviewed your own manager.

- **Clients and Customers**. Seek feedback through conversation or surveys about your strengths and growth areas. This feeds you buzz about your potential traits. Asking customers will also send a message that you want to improve your service to them, which is a great side benefit.

- **Past Associates**. Since people at a former company now have nothing to lose, they might be forthcoming with you about your past buzz. You probably wrapped up your behavior patterns and any related buzz in a package and brought them with you to your new job.

- **Contractors, Suppliers, Vendors, and Consultants**. We sometimes get complacent with our behavior toward those who consider us their clients, so they can serve as a valuable truth serum about our best and worst traits.

- **Mentors**. Since they are usually not in your current chain of command, they can also be candid, especially since that's part of their role.

- **Friends and Family**. This group knows you at your best and worst. They can provide insights into qualities that may transfer to work situations as your corporate buzz.

Listen

Keep your own ear to the ground for what people are saying. Don't hire a gumshoe to wiretap phones or bug associates' cars! But do pick up on perceptions through casual conversation, friendly but revealing jokes, or thinly veiled annoyance. If you take the floor at the end of a meeting at 5:05 p.m. and someone jokes to a neighbor, "Better call in for pizza," it's a safe bet he sees you as a blowhard who will ramble on late into the night. If a team member timidly asks if you really want him to follow protocol to the T, you may be seen as too stuck to red tape, an extreme left-side flaw. If a peer hems and haws before answering your question, you may have a reputation for being aggressive. If a subordinate sighs with exasperation and asks, "Can we please just stick to the core issue and not miss the forest through the trees?," you may suffer from paralysis of analysis. You also probably have low credibility—why else would she ever dare to criticize you?

After you learn the components of your buzz, here's a summary of what you do with this information:

1. Never reinforce negative buzz.

2. If the buzz has some truth to it and it's important (it is a key component to your organization's leadership scorecard or the scorecard for the role you aspire to), improving in this area becomes a top priority.

3. If you think the buzz is more perception than reality, create a visible plan like Maria did to correct perceptions.

So everyone needs to know their buzz, but to complete the picture and enable you to be laser guided as you navigate your organization, you also have to focus on the next rule, Rule 5, the real scorecard.

·· LEADERSHIP PROFILE ··

Silvina Moschini

Silvina is an Argentine entrepreneur who is the founder of Yandiki, She-Works! and Intuic and president of the KMGi Corp. She is an international speaker in the areas of digital innovation, technology, and female entrepreneurship. In 2020 she became the first Latina to bring a company to "unicorn" status and has received the Women in Tech Lifetime Achievement Award. Currently she is probably best known for producing and hosting the increasingly popular show *Unicorn Hunters*.

Raised in a small town in Argentina, in an athletic, competitive family, Silvina believes her involvement with gymnastics generated many of the qualities that have helped her be a successful entrepreneur. She learned the value of discipline and practice, and the mental toughness of dealing with fatigue and pain.

Early in life she remembers having a fierce desire to be financially independent, not having to rely on others. Silvina smiles broadly when she repeats one of her favorite inspirational sayings: "Be the CEO your parents wanted you to marry," which is exactly what she set out to do.

Her educational journey took her to top universities around the world, focusing on the areas of communication, public relations, and public affairs. Amazingly, her first major job involved working for the president of Argentina. So, while in her early twenties, she was meeting kings, queens, and heads of state—and sometimes advising them. This experience helped her become comfortable around power.

In the years that followed, she worked in several communications roles where a key component of her activities involved crisis management. This ability to perform under pressure has been invaluable as an entrepreneur. At a certain point she realized that while she could have continued to navigate organizational power dynamics, her future was not in corporate.

Anyone meeting Silvina recognizes she has many gifts. In particular she is a master of storytelling, creating narratives and making things visible. She strongly believes that "you cannot be what you cannot see."

Through SheWorks!, *Unicorn Hunters*, and her inspirational talks, Silvina is a powerful force training and empowering female entrepreneurs.

◆

Rule 4 Self-Assessment: Know Your Buzz
Score yourself in these five areas, with 1 being "not at all," and 5 being "all the time."

1. I continually assess how I am perceived within the organization, regardless of fairness or accuracy.

      1   2   3   4   5

2. I track the positive and negative traits associated with my work group.

      1   2   3   4   5

3. I tactfully ask the right people about my reputation in the organization.

      1   2   3   4   5

4. I avoid reinforcing any negative buzz.

      1   2   3   4   5

5. I develop a plan to change any perceptions that may harm my team or me.

①   ②   ③   ④   ⑤

Know Your Buzz Action Plans

Use your low scores to guide you toward an action plan.

1. ....

....

2. ....

....

3. ....

....

CHAPTER 8

Rule 5:
Focus on the Real Scorecard

There are several "scorecards" that are important to pay attention to.

The Cultural Scorecard: Every organizational culture has norms, core values, taboos, and success factors. Particularly in organizations that have a long successful past and are proud of their culture, you would do well to think about "cultural fit." Becton, Dickinson and Company (BD), General Mills, and T. Rowe Price are examples of companies where this "fit" is very important.

The Role Scorecard: This consists of the competencies and success factors for your current role and the role you aspire to. Colin Powell, in his autobiography, revealed a career strategy that he feels helped him rise to the highest level of the US armed forces. While focusing on being successful in his current role, he also was intentional about finding out the qualities and skills the army was looking for in the role he wanted next. He then developed and demonstrated those capacities when opportunities arose.

Organizations make bets on people. General Powell stacked the odds in his favor by showcasing components of the role scorecard. This information is available. Usually, human resources has a list of competencies for each role. Sometimes your manager can provide the information. Ask: "Joe, you've done my job. Can you tell me what are the key differences in this role? Time, priorities, key skills?"

The Leadership Scorecard: How do the people in power, the real people who make decisions about your career, define leadership? What are the core values and key competencies they look for in leaders they will elevate? What are the "knockout" factors that eliminate you from consideration for getting more responsibility? This is the most important scorecard to be aware of. The key connection to make is that this leadership scorecard directly translates to people decisions.

I've already mentioned scorecard elements of two famous, highly successful leaders, Larry Bossidy (execution) and Indra Nooyi (strategic acuity). What's significant is that while working extensively in both their organizations (Bossidy, Allied Signal; and Nooyi, PepsiCo), I observed many leadership choices directly related to their scorecard. I could give you hundreds of examples of scorecard issues that determined a woman's career trajectory, but I'm going to provide Sophia's case study because it illustrates how the scorecard relates to your professional development action plan.

Two Scorecards

Twenty years ago I was invited to be the executive coach for a yearlong program designed for high-potential leaders. These leaders met with the CEO, John, and the COO, Eric, each quarter for a two-day offsite. I had individual meetings with the participants during the year and did quarterly check-ins with John and Eric to monitor progress.

About halfway through the program, I had the following conversation about Sophia, one of the participants.

Marty: "John, how is Sophia doing in the program?"

John: "Marty, I really like her approach. She's a very effective collaborator. At meetings, she listens carefully and makes her points after others have weighed in. I like that. She often makes connections to other people's perspectives and actually moves the discussion forward. Very thoughtful. She doesn't talk just to hear herself talk."

Then I called Eric.

Marty: "Eric, how is Sophia doing in the program?"

Eric: "Marty, I'm very disappointed in her. She has more experience and knowledge than the other participants, but she holds back at meetings. I look for and expect "thought leadership" from someone at her level, and I just don't see it. It's not just meetings. Last month I went on a market tour with her and she was invisible. Her team did all the presentations and updates. I want people who lead from the front."

Of course I discussed the feedback with Sophia as soon as possible. She explained to me that several years before, she attended a program offered through her church called Servant Leadership. It was based on the relationship between Jesus and his disciples. She said it resonated with her and she had internalized the values and practices in her approach to leading people. I'm going to give you the ending first. Sophia was able to turn things around with Eric and eventually win his endorsement. But let's take our time and extract all the lessons we can from her situation.

Lesson 1: People will tell you how to sell them. —Tom Hopkins

When John or Eric was giving me information about Sophia, they were giving me very important insights into themselves. This is a principle I use extensively in my work, and you can use to rapidly assess someone's scorecard. I asked them an open-ended question. They responded from their inner framework. They chose what to focus on and revealed what they like and what bothers them.

So just to summarize this key point, when John and Eric were talking about Sophia, they were equally talking about themselves.

Lesson 2: Attributions

People can agree about someone's behavior and still have very different explanations about the motives for that behavior—what they attribute it to. John attributes Sophia's behavior at meetings to a desire to listen, understand, collaborate, and align. Eric attributes her behavior to a lack of "thought leadership" or conviction. So the scorecard can often determine whether the attribution will help you or hurt you.

Lesson 3: Flexing My Leadership Style: The Difference between Phony/Inauthentic versus Uncomfortable

Let's use everything we've learned so far to guide Sophia through the process of absorbing the feedback and deciding what to do.

Rule 1: Study Power

If John, the CEO, had the power and would use it, Sophia might not have had to change much at all. However, she shared that John was probably going to retire soon, and Eric was his likely successor. In any case, John usually deferred to Eric on people decisions in his organization, and Sophia reported to Eric.

Rule 4: Know Your Buzz and Rule 5: Focus on the Scorecard

It was clear to both of us that given Eric's scorecard, Sophia would top out in his organization unless she could change his view of her. Does she want to do that, and could she do it in a way that doesn't conflict with her values?

Some of you may be thinking, Servant Leadership is a respected approach to people; it fits her values and it's effective for her, so why should she change? She should be authentic and true to herself. Sometimes there is a real values conflict between your moral compass and the scorecard. What I recommend is first trying to see if there is a way to maintain your values while still demonstrating the key capacities in the scorecard.

This is what Sophia did. Before all meetings and conference calls with Eric, Sophia prepared extensively. Her goal was to enter the conversation with "natural conviction," a strong point of view on the agenda topics. This made it easier for her to speak earlier in meetings and to speak with more conviction, using phrases such as:

"My point of view . . ."

"I recommend . . ."

"If this were my decision, I would . . ."

"Based on my experience with these kinds of challenges I would . . ."

It also prepared her to stand her ground if people pushed back on her positions.

She also revised her process for market tours with Eric. She took the lead in the tours and presentations and was still able to showcase the contributions and insights of her team.

So let's look at the issue of being "authentic" versus being "uncomfortable." If Sophia had said things she didn't believe, exaggerated or distorted information, started talking in a loud voice, interrupted people, or not given her team any visibility on market tours, then yes, she would have been inauthentic. But the action plan she developed, which involved only about 5 percent of her time, consisted of behaviors that were "uncomfortable" but not in conflict with her values. I know that "be authentic" is popular leadership and personal advice. I think it's good advice as long as we keep this distinction in mind: phony/inauthentic versus uncomfortable.

Scorecard Exercises

To test your understanding of the scorecard and its connection to career risk, here are five scenarios to evaluate. I define *career risk* as the potential for lack of alignment with the scorecard to cause you to plateau or derail.

1. Marcy

   Marcy is a polite and trusting person. She believes she should treat people the way that she wants to be treated. Recently, her division was acquired by a company whose executives are much more aggressive, competitive, and political.

   Marcy Career Risk

   | Low | Moderate | High |

   This is a situation where the scorecard is about to change in a way that is quite unfavorable to Marcy. Her strengths are likely to be devalued, and she will probably need to quickly become more forceful and organizationally savvy.

   But should she? Individuals will answer this question differently. I would advise Marcy that even if she eventually decides the organization is no longer right for her, she can use this as an opportunity to acquire toughness and savvy, which will be useful to her wherever she ends up.

2. Robert

   Robert regularly has emotional outbursts, which include yelling at people in meetings. He also has an outstanding track record of consistently high performance. Recently, two of his direct reports have complained to human resources about his disrespectful and intimidating behavior. Robert's manager puts performance over any other quality in evaluating leaders. He also believes "great" leaders are feared, not loved.

   Robert Career Risk

   | Low | Moderate | High |

   Even though many of us would like Robert's career risk to be high, under the circumstances described, it actually isn't. Based on his manager's scorecard, Robert's strengths are highly valued and his negatives, short of a lawsuit, don't matter.

I included this scenario to help you understand situations in your organization where there seem to be no consequences for bad behavior or performance.

3. Simon

Simon is a sensitive and empathetic leader. He has a high need for affiliation and building connections with people. Due to a recent organizational shift, he is the new leader of an underperforming team. He has been told that there are several marginal performers on the team and widespread dysfunctional behavior. His manager has told him that after thirty days of evaluating people and the situation, he expects Simon to have some "tough love" conversations and change out some team members.

Simon Career Risk

Low   Moderate   High

This is a situation where the scorecard (tough love, timely people decisions) is clearly aligned with achieving performance goals. Someone like Simon is usually very responsible, and if he can see that developing these skills (even if uncomfortable) is what the team needs, he will be motivated to change. He will need to see that someone can be tough and also fair and respectful.

4. Todd

Todd is a marketing executive with exceptional relationship-building skills and a wide network, which includes media contacts. Often, he is able to obtain publicity for the company and products and is often quoted in business journals. The new CEO of his company is a very modest person with a very low need for attention or visibility. He tends to label people who call attention to themselves as "self-serving" or "self-promoters, not team players."

Todd Career Risk

Low   Moderate   High

I would put the risk here as moderate. Todd definitely needs to study the new CEO's scorecard and adjust his behavior accordingly. He can still achieve his publicity goals but should make sure the articles reflect "we, not me."

5. Gabriella

Gabriella is a long-tenured executive with strong process and project management skills. She tends to micromanage, believing that her way is THE way to approach projects. There has been a lot of change and a dramatic increase in complexity in her industry. Because of this, her manager has pressured her to hire younger, more creative, "disruptive" thinkers, which she has done.

Gabriella Career Risk

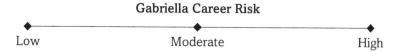

Low   Moderate   High

I included Gabriella's situation to introduce the idea of "rising" risk. Up to now, Gabriella has been a "safe pair of hands," a reliable performer. How do you think a young, looking-around-corners person, who has many choices about where to work, will react to being instructed about "the way of doing things"? With no flexing on Gabriella's part, there is a good chance one of these highly sought-after hires will not stick around. So this shift in the industry and type of new hires is a "rising" career risk to Gabriella.

In sum, focusing on the real scorecard helps you make decisions on:

- how to prioritize your time
- what you communicate about
- what you include in your individual development plan

.... LEADERSHIP PROFILE ....
Susan Morris

Susan Morris is the chief operations officer for Albertsons Companies, the second largest supermarket chain in North America, with over 2,300 grocery stores and 275,000 employees.

She started to work in one of their stores as a way to pay for college, and thirty-plus years later, she is still with the company, having risen to the top of her industry. In 2020 she received the Top Woman in Grocery Trailblazer award.

Susan's leadership style is an effective blend of internal collaboration and external customer focus; she both empowers her teams and holds them accountable. One quality that endears her to so many people at Albertsons is that she treats everyone the same. From CEO Vivek Sankaran and the board to employees in the warehouses and stores, she treats others with fairness and respect, and returns their loyalty. She is also devoted to mentoring and empowering female leaders and is the executive sponsor of Albertsons' Women Inclusion and Inspiration Network (WIIN).

At a WIIN forum for hundreds of women in April 2021, Susan shared how she has leveraged some of the 12 Rules in her career journey, particularly Rule 5, Know the Real Scorecard. She explained that because she has worked for only one company, in only one industry, she began to assume the following:

- There was no need to self-promote because everyone knew who she was and what she had accomplished.
- She had a thorough knowledge of what it took to be successful, both at Albertsons and in the industry.

While, of course, many of these success factors remained priorities, Rule 5 alerted her to the implications of Vivek being brought in as the new CEO. For example, the power dynamics shifted as human resources became a key partner to Vivek. Through observation and being open to feedback, she also realized that the scorecard—the lens through which she was being evaluated—had changed. While retaining all of her strengths and best practices, Susan also focused on her executive presence and enhanced her "ability to spot ability," that is, evaluate and upgrade talent.

In these past two years, Susan has grown as a leader, providing guidance and inspiration during the COVID-19 pandemic and running the businesses at record volumes while protecting the well-being of Albertsons' employees and customers.

◆

Rule 5 Self-Assessment: Focus on the Real Scorecard

Score yourself in these five areas, with 1 being "not at all," and 5 being "all the time."

1. I am aware of the leadership scorecard that is used to evaluate me.

①   ②   ③   ④   ⑤

2. I know the key attributes my organization is looking for in the roles I aspire to.

①   ②   ③   ④   ⑤

3. Through observation and my network, I can identify the taboos of key leaders in my organization.

①   ②   ③   ④   ⑤

4. By knowing my buzz and the scorecard, I can determine my key professional development objectives.

①   ②   ③   ④   ⑤

5. I stay current regarding the priorities and shifting priorities of people in power.

①   ②   ③   ④   ⑤

Focus on the Real Scorecard Action Plans

Use your low scores to guide you toward an action plan.

1. ....

....

2. ....

....

3. ....

....

CHAPTER 9

Rule 6: Leverage Your Network

The day you need a network, it's too late to build it.

I'll start this Rule 6 discussion with a very strong statement. No matter how hard you work and how good your results are, you won't reach your full career potential without building *and* leveraging your network. In this chapter I'm going to share the 11 essential ways a network can help you, but first I'll illustrate the power of a network with a personal example.

I've been an executive coach for 35 years and at about my 10-year mark, I had a fairly solid record after coaching about 600 people. I had no retainers or guarantees, but I was feeling confident about my position, particularly with my major client. One Friday afternoon I got a call from someone in my network (Person #1) at that company. (I always remember it was a Friday because I spent the weekend thinking about what I was going to do after I lost my biggest client!)

Network Person #1 said, "Marty, go to your fax machine and make sure you are sitting down. I'm sending you a letter about you that is circulating in the company."

> **To**: All Senior Vice Presidents of Human Resources [all the people who hired me for coaching engagements]
>
> **From**: David G [VP of leadership development: At the request of Roger L [head of HR for the entire company and the second most powerful person at the company]
>
> **Subject**: Marty Seldman
>
> Roger has asked me to investigate Marty Seldman's "fix it" program. Please provide information about his results and how much your di-

vision pays him every year. In 10 days I'll publish the results of this investigation.

My Reaction: Wow! ROGER L, SELDMAN, FIXIT PROGRAM, MONEY, INVESTIGATE, all in one email.

After receiving this, I wondered who would want to work with me. Luckily someone in my network had given me a heads-up only hours after this happened, so I decided to "get there early" and take my own advice by leveraging my network. Here's what unfolded.

Network Person #2 said, "Marty, I was at the meeting when this got started. Roger likes to know how much consultants make, and he asked how much money you make a year. He never used the word *investigate*."

This was very valuable information because it revealed that David had a hidden agenda, but I still didn't know what it was, so I kept digging.

Network Person #3 said, "David just spent $4 million of the company's money on an outside group that developed an ideal leadership profile. They also do executive coaching and he wants to bring them in to justify the investment. But right now you are in his way."

Several other HR leaders who received the letter went to Roger and supported me. The hidden agenda was confirmed when the findings turned out to be positive. David never published them.

So I survived thanks to my network providing timely information and standing up for me. David's plan could easily have worked. The only thing he underestimated was my network.

I continued to work for that client for an additional 20 years. David G left the company six months after he sent the letter. (I swear, I had nothing to do with his departure!)

11 Potential Benefits of a Network

I'm providing this list both to motivate you to build a network and to pinpoint for you exactly what advantages it can provide.

1. **Provides feedback/buzz.** Most people will be more candid with your network than they will be with you directly.

2. **Helps you study power.** Your network has information about meetings, remarks, and people decisions that provide key insights about power.

3. **Detects to protect.** Remember Francoise (page 48) in the case

study involving Anne. She was giving Anne information about an overly political person, based on patterns of behavior.

4. **Catches someone taking credit for your ideas or your results.** Your network will hear about it way before you will.

5. **Alerts you to efforts at blaming or sabotage.** The same logic applies here. As in my personal example, time matters. The early warning gives you more opportunity to protect yourself.

6. **Helps sell your ideas.** People in your network are often in a position to advance your ideas. The most valuable of these is the internal advocate, for example, the finance person who can persuade the CFO much more effectively than you can.

7. **Promotes your accomplishments.** Your network has dozens of forums and platforms to share your results, learnings, and how you made progress.

8. **Stands up for you.** Hopefully you rarely need this, but as you saw in my situation, although it was only once in 10 years, it was a make-or-break event.

9. **Exposes hidden agendas.** There are ways you can spot the presence of a hidden agenda (see Rule 10, page 115), but often someone in your network knows exactly what the agenda is.

10. **Provides emotional support/validation.** Every morning, I spend time in gratitude, especially focusing on people who have loved me and guided me. The woman who had the biggest impact on my life did it by reassuring me, "No, Marty, you are not crazy." Sometimes we just need people to listen, to empathize with, and validate our feelings. People at work actually can be in a better position to do this than our friends and family because they are aware of the workplace realities.

11. **Takes the target off your back.** Let's say there is an overly political person in your organization who unfortunately is skillful at "managing the airwaves," blaming others, creating negative buzz, and marginalizing. Who are they going to target? Is it someone with a wide, active, powerful network who will quickly help them see the threat coming and use their power and access to stand up for you? They might, but there is a lot of risk because the target will shoot back. They are more likely to go after someone they are not afraid of, someone who won't see it coming.

How to Build Your Network

Hopefully I've motivated you to build and maintain you network. There are many books and guides on the subject of networking, but here are four components to keep top of mind.

1. **Building Relationships:** Recent global studies revealed that senior management ranked female employees more highly on:

   - motivating and engaging others
   - empathic listening
   - building strong teams
   - negotiating win-wins
   - building morale

   So use your relationship-building skills, your listening, and curiosity to learn about other people's interests, circumstances, and goals.

2. **Targeted Networking:** Julia Johnson, an executive coach, says, "In my observation, when men build relationships at work, they're usually very focused. They pursue people they believe can help them accomplish their objectives. Women often have multiple reasons for developing relationships." So in the limited time you have to network, go beyond the people you are comfortable with or collaborate with. Targets for your network include:

   - If you are in the field, someone in headquarters
   - If there are power functions in your organizations (finance, marketing), someone from those functions
   - People who have access to and influence on power
   - People who are "wired in" and always seem to know what is going on in the organization
   - People you can learn from
   - Mentors and sponsors

3. **Creating Opportunities**
   - When you go on business trips and attend conferences or meetings, set up time in advance to spend with key people.

- You probably eat lunch every day, so why not combine it with networking?
- Speaking of combining, you can network while power walking, working out at the company gym, or volunteering at Habitat for Humanity.

4. **Quid Pro Quo:** You can't build a sustainable network by approaching people with the line, "I'm here today because Marty recommended that I build a network." A strong network consists of a mutual exchange of benefits, a quid pro quo. Review the 11 benefits. They point to what you can offer people in your network. In addition, I always am aware of other ways I can add value, for example, by sending articles; making introductions; recommending experts in health care, financial or legal matters; helping my network's family members. Most of these actions take very little time but are much appreciated and long remembered.

Overcoming Reluctance

In their book *How Women Rise*, Sally Helgesen and Marshall Goldsmith devote considerable space to discussing why women are often reluctant to pursue the benefits of their network.

They found that many women are held back by concerns that they will be seen as "pushy," "out for themselves," or "using people." So I want to share several ways many women have been able to coach themselves to overcome these reluctances.

1. *"I would do this for people in my network if they asked me. I have already, without being asked, done these types of actions for people in my network."* This is a reminder of how using the network can be mutually beneficial versus self-serving.

2. *"My interests are aligned with the company's interests and consistent with our values."* This also counters the self-censorship causing the reluctance.

3. *"I can't lose what I don't have."* Right now you may not have people selling your ideas, promoting your accomplishments, or standing up for you. If you ask for this kind of support from them and they say no, you are simply back where you started. You have everything to gain by asking, including that many, many people love to help others and feel a strong bond with people they help.

Paula's CEO Perspective

"You have to build a network before your need it." I heard this phrase from Marty when I was a young executive. The statement was followed by very clear examples of when entire businesses had been saved by a timely use of network information. Often, people are saved by their network. Or, put another way, people are damaged if they don't have one. Women are sometimes blissfully unaware of how important it is to build a network, considering it a waste of time. After all, we are super busy trying to achieve our objectives. That alone is a day job, without mentioning we are most likely also raising a family. Why would we need to worry about building a network? No time. Not a priority. Wrong. You are wrong. It is a massive personal priority. I have seen women fail over and over again because they have not built a timely network.

One day, I was mentoring a young executive who wanted to grow in our organization. She wanted a career change. We discussed options. Every time I said someone's name, her response was that she had never met them. So, we built a list of about 12 individuals she could contact to promote herself and her desire to grow within our organization. After getting about halfway through the list, she came back into my office exclaiming, "I know nobody. Nobody knows me. I am perfectly invisible to everyone in this company. I am a corporate ghost!" She had developed keen awareness that she had not invested the time in getting to know people inside the company she worked for! Imagine her network outside the company. It was even worse.

It does take time to build a good network. You need to build it purposefully and strategically. This means creating a really good list of strategic individuals you want to build a trustworthy relationship with. Once you have the list, invite them to a coffee, lunch, or a Zoom session. Have a 30-minute free-ranging conversation. Prepare a few questions. Women sometimes do not recognize that this is as important to you as it is to the other individual. It goes both ways. So if your list is sharply thought out, you will most likely find mutual interest in building a stronger relationship.

♦

Rule 6 Self-Assessment: Leverage Your Network

Score yourself in these five areas, with 1 being "not at all," and 5 being "all the time."

1. I build and maintain positive relationships through an informal network in the organization.

    ① ② ③ ④ ⑤

2. I create allies and advocates who will support my proposals and ideas.

    ① ② ③ ④ ⑤

3. I efficiently and graciously mix with many people at large corporate events.

    ① ② ③ ④ ⑤

4. I stay involved in cross-organizational activities such as task forces, committees, cross-functional teams, and professional affiliations.

    ① ② ③ ④ ⑤

5. I make sure my network includes the people who are most informed about what is happening in the organization.

    ① ② ③ ④ ⑤

Leverage Your Network Action Plans

Use your low scores to guide you toward an action plan.

1. ....

   ....

2. ....

   ....

3. ....

   ....

CHAPTER 10

Rule 7:
Increase Your Value
to the Organization

A s you have already gleaned from reading the case studies and stories, being an executive coach has given me insight into what sociologists call "the hidden dialogue" of organizational life.

These insights—combined with the data gained from tracking thousands of careers—revealed that there was often no guarantee that an organization would make an informed decision about your capabilities or that you would get the credit or recognition you deserve. Rules 1 to 6 are aimed at addressing those issues. Rule 7 focuses on the "deserve" part. Hopefully your career is built on a solid foundation: strong work ethic, integrity, focus on results, collaboration, and expertise in knowledge or process.

Now we are going to look at building on that foundation to add three qualities—strategic thinking skills, being a quick study, and focusing on the "top of the list"—that earn you consideration for bigger roles and a positive career protectory.

Strategic Thinking Skills

Modern organizational life is characterized by rapid, disruptive change, increasing complexity, and being "crazy busy." In that environment, simply being good at a certain way of operating or a "safe pair of hands" may give you some job security, but the broader roles will go to people who look ahead and anticipate change.

Strategic thinking is a very broad term, like *leadership*. You can rarely be sure what someone means when they describe a person as "strategic" unless they get more specific.

In my work this term was used so often that I decided to do interviews to pinpoint exactly what term meant and, more importantly, what organizations were looking for. The result is the Strategic Thinking scorecard.

Strategic Thinking Scorecard	My Competence (1–10)	How am I Perceived (1–10)
1. Longer-Term Focus (vs. tactical/operational)		
2. Broad-Based Perspective/Systems Thinking (vs. functional/ subject matter expert)		
3. Innovative and/or Fosters Innovation		
4. "Looking Around Corners"		
5. Strategic Concepts/Language		
6. Micro and Macro		

I suggest that you score yourself (from 1 to 10) in two ways for each of the six items. The competence score reflects your ability in this area. The perception score points to how you think the organization would rate you in this area.

1. **Longer-Term Focus (versus Tactical/Operational).** Are you looking down the road a year, two years, longer? How will what you are doing now position you in 18 months? How will it position you for what the competition is planning? Do other people know you are planning long term, or do they see you as tactical/operational?

2. **Broad-Based Perspective/Systems Thinking (versus Functional/ Subject Matter Expertise).** Does the organization see you as "narrow" or "staying in your lane"? Or do they understand that you have a working knowledge of the other functions and how the marketplace works as an integrated system?

3. **Innovative and/or Fosters Innovation.** Do you demonstrate a willingness to try new things, bring in innovative ideas, and encourage the creativity of the people around you?

4. **"Looking Around Corners."** People demonstrate this ability by being curious and paying close attention to trends and change. They think through varieties of scenarios and reflect on the possible implications of change.

5. **Strategic Concepts/Language.** Senior leadership in your organi-

zation probably has their favorite strategy gurus, books, or management consulting companies. Are you familiar with the concepts and language they frequently use (e.g., *blue ocean, white space, adjacent/core, competitive intent,* etc.)?

6. **Micro and Macro.** The most valuable strategic thinkers are the ones whose strategies are realistic and practical. So the best plans combine macro (higher-level strategic concepts) with the micro (how things really work at the consumer, delivery-of-services, or manufacturing level). Do you combine the macro and the micro in your strategic plans and presentations?

If your competence scores are low in any of the six components, there are ways to improve:

- Read the *Harvard Business Review*, which usually contains the latest trends in strategic thinking.
- Find out about and read the books favored by senior management and the management consultants they have.
- Seek out people in your organization who excel in these areas.
- Enroll in onsite and online university programs on strategic thinking.
- Set aside time for reflection and think about the changes/trends you are noticing and hearing about.

If your perception score is significantly lower than your competence score, it's a sign that you are not marketing your strategic thinking—often an issue involving self-promotion. Rule 8 will provide many tips for closing this gap.

Being a Quick Study

A quick study is someone who demonstrates the ability to rapidly ascend the learning curve in new situations. If this is part of your buzz, that's very good news. Since rapid change is guaranteed, organizations have more confidence that a quick study will have the agility and confidence to adapt.

Here are some of the positive qualities that are attributed to a quick study.

- **Curiosity.** They are not anxious about change; they demonstrate curiosity and interest in it.

- **Confidence.** They can admit they have skill deficits and gaps in their knowledge. But they are very confident in their ability to learn.
- **Urgency.** They understand that being slow to adapt or figure out solutions may eliminate the possibility of prevailing in competitive situations. So they seek out information and insights with urgency.
- **Proactive.** This is one of the most attractive traits of a "Quick Study." He or she doesn't need to be told or guided. A "Quick Study" will proactively do the reading and research, and/or contact people they can learn from.
- **Risk-taking.** A quick study has high standards but is not as concerned about "mistakes" as most people. Because they are intently focused on learning, they are constantly moving forward.

Are you a quick study? If so, is this part of your buzz? Are there aspects of being a quick study that you could improve on?

Focusing on the "Top of the List"

When someone remarks that someone else works the "top of the list," it is usually a compliment. It implies that this person is clear about their top priorities, meaning their high-payoff activities, and that's where they place their focus and effort.

If you remember, I shared the key advantage men gain by committing to projects that align with the senior management scorecard and/or top priorities. By studying power and gathering information from your network, you can zero in on those priorities (for example, margins, market share, cost cutting, collaboration, innovation, customer service, competitive advantage, and so on). Focusing on the top of the list means using this knowledge to guide your choices about how you spend your time and what you say yes to. What you focus on in your work, what projects you sign up for, what you read, and how you leverage your network can add value to these key priorities. These actions gather positive attention and appreciation from key leaders, elevating your profile in the organization.

So strategic thinking, being a quick study, and focusing on the top of the list will increase your value to your organization *only if* these attributes are recognized. To make sure that happens we need to be prepared to do at least a minimum amount of self-promotion. This is not easy for some of us, thus Rule 8.

······················ LEADERSHIP PROFILE ··················

Srijana Karki

Srijana Karki is the regional director of South Asia for World Neighbors (WN), guiding WN projects in India and Nepal and coordinating with government officials, donors, and other NGOs. Every year the programs improve the lives of tens of thousands of people in small communities and rural areas. The approach to empowering rural women and small farmers is holistic and opens doors to sustainable agriculture, economic self-reliance, and reproductive health, plus water and sanitation.

Srijana was raised in Kathmandu, Nepal. She doesn't remember seeing any women in power or leadership positions and didn't have a mentor or sponsor growing up. Somehow, though, she was imbued with a strong feeling of independence. She was rebellious and insisted on participating in the same activities as the boys in her family and community. This was accomplished by a fierce determination not to be defined or confined by her culture.

A major decision, which put her on the road to independence, was to go to university. She made this decision without consulting her family. Her educational journey included an MBA from Nepal's Tribhuvan University. After her MBA, she worked at a variety of roles but lacked passion and purpose.

At that point she was exposed to efforts groups were making to empower rural communities. She was impressed by the women she met who were committed to bettering the lives of their families and communities.

It has been said that the two most important days in your life are the day you are born and the day you find out why you were born. Srijana discovered why she was born: she committed to raising women's voices. This has allowed her to witness the transition of women who initially were afraid to speak up in their own families, yet they developed the courage and skill to represent their village in discussions with government officials.

Although Srijana didn't grow up with female role models, she has become one. Recently she was visiting a village where one of the women participating in the project work had recently given birth to a daughter. When Srijana arrived, the new mother asked her if she would touch the baby—because she wanted her to grow up to be a leader like Srijana.

··· ◆ ···

Rule 7 Self-Assessment: Increase Your Value to the Organization

Score yourself in these five areas, with 1 being "not at all," and 5 being "all the time."

1. I think through the longer-term implications of my current plans and objectives.

   (1)   (2)   (3)   (4)   (5)

2. I take an enterprise-wide view regarding the impact of my function's activities.

   (1)   (2)   (3)   (4)   (5)

3. I stay current with the strategic models and concepts used by senior leaders in my organization.

   (1)   (2)   (3)   (4)   (5)

4. I retain my curiosity and openness to learning.

   (1)   (2)   (3)   (4)   (5)

5. I realize that I need to be agile and ready to acquire new skills and knowledge.

   (1)   (2)   (3)   (4)   (5)

Increase Your Value to the Organization Action Plans

Use your low scores to guide you toward an action plan.

1. ....

....

2. ....

....

3. ....

....

CHAPTER 11

Rule 8:
Promote Yourself with
Decent Boldness

If I am not for myself, who will be?
If I am not only for myself, what am I?
If not now, when?
—The Talmud

Modest	Let the Results Speak for Themselves	Effective Self-Promotion	Excessive Self-Promotion	Exaggerating Achievements

Self-Promotion Continuum

As you read about the range of attributes and behaviors along the self-promotion continuum, assess where you tend to operate from.

Modest: This person has a low need for attention, visibility, or recognition and may even get uncomfortable with public praise.

Let the Results Speak for Themselves: Someone with this approach puts their focus and effort on achievement. They believe in fairness and that at the end of the day a meritocracy will prevail and the most deserving people will be rewarded.

Effective Self-Promotion: This is the goal of Rule 8. The foundation is built on effort and achievement, while recognizing that additional steps are often required to ensure that their work is recognized and credited to them. They find ways to do this in an authentic way that is consistent with their values.

Excessive Self-Promotion: Based on cultural and organizational norms, this person is calling attention to themselves too often and/or overly bragging about their results.

Exaggerating Achievements: Here we are in a dangerous area because achievements are being exaggerated, people are overpromising, or the wrong people are being credited and rewarded.

What influences our views/values regarding self-promotion?

- **Geography/Culture.** I grew up in Brooklyn, New York, where bragging was so normal that it was expected. At the age of 20 I moved to Japan, where saying something nice about yourself is a serious cultural taboo. What were the norms about this behavior where you were raised?

- **Religious Messages.** Many of the world's major religions emphasize the importance of humility ("hide your light under a bushel").

- **Family Values.** If your parents often denigrated people who promoted themselves, using comments such as *conceited, cocky, arrogant, full of himself, talks a good game,* and *braggart,* it's easy to develop an aversion to being perceived in these ways.

- **Gender/Gender Expectations.** Of course, we all know women who are very effective at promoting themselves and men who struggle in this area, but here the results are quite clear. Deborah Tannen, an expert in gender communication, executive coaches like Lois Frankel, Nila Betof, Sally Helgesen, Marshall Goldsmith, and I have consistently found that, in general, men are more comfortable talking about, and even bragging about their accomplishments.

So why are many women reluctant to promote themselves?

As we saw with reluctance to leveraging your network, women are often concerned about being perceived negatively, or going against their values. They don't want to be viewed as self-centered, pushy, "saleswomen," conceited, or having a "me versus we" approach. This attitude is captured well in a quote from *How Women Rise.* Helgesen and Goldsmith interviewed a woman who said, "If I have to act like that obnoxious blowhard down the hall to get noticed around here, I'd prefer to be ignored. I have no desire to behave like that jerk."

Additionally, many women believe in fairness and meritocracy, so they are not doing enough to make their contributions visible because they think they shouldn't have to. This can actually work well for a while if their manager is informing the organization and/or their results are clearly measurable and visible.

So now the objectives of Rule 8 are clear: we need to find an approach that is compatible with a person's values and self-image, while avoiding the risks of too little self-promotion. We discussed these risks previously, but I want to review them and flesh them out here before we focus on the skills we will need.

> **Being Underestimated.** We have seen that because the people who will make decisions about your career are so busy, it is possible they won't know about results or credit them to your ideas and initiative. They also may simply not know key information about your background, education, or capabilities. After a seminar I taught on this subject, a woman approached me and said, "You know, when you were talking, I had a revelation. I have four master's degrees and I realize no one who works with me knows that."

Early in my career I found myself in a similar situation. In the first 10 years of my career I had trained over a thousand training seminar leaders. But when I went to work for my first major client, it was as an executive coach. After working there for a few years, I noticed that when I talked to my clients about coaching they were engaged, but when I talked to them about training, their eyes would glaze over. Finally, the simple, ironic reality dawned on me. I knew I had trained a thousand trainers, but the clients had no way of knowing that unless I told them!

> **False Attributions.** Sometimes I have seen people get overall credit for a result, but the attribution or explanation for the result is inaccurate and unfavorable. For example, you get credit for completing a project but they attribute the success to "how hard you work" instead of the strategic thinking and planning you did. Or they credit you with good collaboration skills but attribute the "Strategic Thinking" to someone else on your team.

Other People Take—and Get—Credit for Your Ideas and Successes. Unfortunately this happens more often than it should. If there is an overly political person in your organization who is not that competent but who is good at "managing the airwaves," you become an easy target. They notice that you have a low need for attention/visibility, that you don't like to self-promote, or that you haven't branded, documented, or socialized your work.

Sometimes it doesn't even take someone with low integrity and bad intentions. Sociologists have documented the phenomenon of *biased social accounting*. This means that many people's memories are favorably biased toward themselves. They may actually forget your role or contribution or that it was your idea. In their memory they exaggerate their impact and may actually believe they were the originators of your brilliant insights.

All these risks are displayed in a case study I would like you to read and analyze. Let's see what we can learn from Amy's lack of self-promotion.

Amy is director of the Consumer Insight group for a $3 billion division of a multinational food company. Her areas of focus are traditional aspects of market research with particular emphasis on tapping into consumer sentiment.

She reports to the senior VP of Marketing, who reports to the CEO. Amy is very bright, with great technical skills and can be persistent if she thinks an idea will help the company. Usually, though, she is fairly quiet, polite, and modest. Her need for individual attention or visibility is low, and she is often fairly quiet at meetings. In one-on-one situations or with smaller groups after meetings, she is more vocal about her ideas.

The CEO, Sam, is well known throughout all divisions of the multinational. He is charismatic, a great speaker, and perceived to be one of the true innovators in the company. It is common knowledge at the division headquarters that Sam is a master of self-promotion. There are several well-known instances where he has exaggerated results or his contribution to results.

Amy's latest research indicates that consumers want the company to package its food in larger portions. With this increased perception of "value" bringing customers into stores, Amy feels this strategy will dramatically increase profits on value items and other products.

Her first two attempts to present her results and strategy to Sam are not successful. In fact he is impatient and dismissive. However, Amy is so sure she is right that she persists, and finally Sam agrees to a test market for her approach.

The test market results are excellent and soon this strategy is rolled out to the entire division. The positive impact on sales and profits is so great that at the end of the year Sam is named executive of the year.

At first Amy felt tremendous pride and satisfaction because her idea had such a dramatic effect on the division. At internal meetings Sam would reference her research, but she began to notice that Sam often implied that the initial impetus to do the research came from him. This became even more noticeable after Amy's boss, the VP of Marketing, was transferred to another division.

Although somewhat upset, Amy comforted herself with the thought that Sam wasn't always precise with words but he surely remembered her insights and persistence. In fact, she expected to be promoted to vice president, since she had already been director for three years and in several of the other divisions her function was headed by a VP.

Recently, though, two events unsettled her.

- One of her peers (Jack) in another division called her to say he was surprised that at a speech to his division, Sam didn't mention Amy or her research. Jack said that Sam made it seem like the strategy was mostly "intuitive."
- Next, her new boss told her that he was too new to evaluate her or recommend her for a VP, so he was deferring her appraisal to Sam.

Finally, Amy met with Sam in what was a disappointing, almost devastating session. The bottom line was that while Sam appreciated her contributions, he couldn't at the time recommend her for a promotion. He said that she needed to work on her leadership style and personal intensity. He went on to say that she did not show "thought leadership" at meetings.

At the end, Sam added that because he personally cared about Amy and she was valuable to the company, he was going to obtain the services of an executive coach to help her with her style.

Case Study Questions and Analysis

1. What errors of omission did Amy make?
2. Using any insights you have about her personality and values, why did she make these mistakes?
3. What are some of the actions she could have taken to protect herself and get credit for her work?
4. What should she do now?

To compound how unfair this turn of events was, Amy's consumer insights, persistence, and "value strategy" leapfrogged her company to become an industry leader. When it was spun off a few years later, it was valued at $10 billion—but Amy got no credit.

We can see that Amy had all the risk factors for not getting credit for her work: modesty, belief that her results would speak for themselves, and trust in Sam and her bosses to "do the right thing."

Trust is valuable when it is earned and deserved, but misplaced trust never leads to anything good. Clearly Amy ignored or rationalized some warning signals. In fact, when I met her, she felt so betrayed that she quit the organization six months after this happened.

What could Amy have done, consistent with her values, to protect herself and her ideas?

Amy was part of a multidivisional company, with a Consumer Insights counterpart in each division. At the first opportunity, a quarterly meeting of her peers, she should have requested a 30-minute presentation on her division's new "value strategy." As part of her presentation to her peers, she would say:

"Each of you has in front of you a printout of the numbers, indicating how the rollout of the value strategy is driving our volume and profits. But today, I want to go beyond the numbers and talk to you about what we are learning: our insights into the consumer about price points, perceptions of value, and about how volume impacts margins. The people who buy our products are the same ones who buy your drinks and snacks. So I want to discuss with you what we have learned about these consumers and talk about how these learnings could potentially be leveraged in your divisions."

By giving this presentation, Amy would have set herself up for applying the following rules.

1. **Leveraging Her Network.** The presentation would have allowed Amy to get the word out to her network *early*. If Sam came around talking about it, people would have responded, "Yes, we heard about how Amy's consumer insights translated into that strategy for the stores."

2. **Branding Her Idea.** Giving your work a name tremendously increases the chances that it will be associated with you. Unfortunately, Sam is the one who did that. At Harvard Business School, where they have a case study on the "value strategy," Sam still gets the credit, even though he twice rejected the idea.

3. **Organizational Learning.** In *The Fifth Discipline*, Peter Senge stated, "The only sustainable competitive advantage is to learn faster than your competitor." Ever since that best seller was published, the value of organizational learning has been widely recognized and people are very receptive to ideas presented under that umbrella. The key is, for someone like Amy, using this framework doesn't feel like bragging and isn't received as bragging. Yet it achieves the desired impact of organizational recognition of Amy's contributions and capabilities. Even more, if any of the other divisions successfully implemented her ideas, her value to the broader company would be magnified.

4. **Promoting Herself with Decent Boldness.** The "decent" part of Amy's presentation refers to the fact that she didn't arrogantly tell other people how to run their business. She made a logical case, explaining why what she had learned could potentially be useful to them. The "boldness" part was her belief in herself, her belief that she could add value and that what she had to say was important. To use a popular phrase, "her truth."

Organizational Learning

To be able to use organizational learning for effective self-promotion, you need to take these steps:

1. Analyze Success

Most people put a lot more time, energy, and focus into analyzing their mistakes and failures. This can be useful, but success has a template that shows us how to replicate it, learn from it, and share the learnings. That is the meaning of the saying, "A professional is not just someone who is good; they know why they are good." So when you and your team make progress and achieve positive results, spend time discovering the elements and steps that brought those results.

2. **Extract the Learnings**

   One reason we want to nail down this success formula is so that we remember to use it again. The second is that we can solidify the learnings for sharing more broadly.

3. **Consider the Implications of the Learnings**

   Think through who else in the organization would be interested in or benefit from these learnings. Then, with decent boldness, share the learnings with confidence and passion, while listening to and respecting others. In addition, I will point out how some of the tips and techniques in Rules 9 and 10 also align with effective self-promotion.

Have a Clear, Accurate Picture of Your Strengths

Remember Shonda Rhimes's statement at the awards ceremony: "I totally deserve this award." It demonstrates more than a comfort with self-promotion; it shows that she has an accurate estimation of her talent. Having a full catalog of your strengths is a key component to feeling confident and dispelling "impostor syndrome," which undermines many women.

Actually, most of us, male and female, don't fully internalize our range of strengths. Here are some of the reasons why:

1. We don't want to be perceived as "arrogant," "conceited," or "full of ourselves." As we have already seen, the same concerns that inhibit someone from self-promotion also hold them back from thinking about and focusing on their strengths.

2. We have lack of clarity about what qualifies as a strength, which leads to us discounting strengths. Many times people are not sure what to count as a strength. Let's look at some of the types of questions that come up:

   Do I have a strength if I know someone who is better than me?
   The correct and helpful answer is yes. You can have a strength even if someone is stronger than you in that ability. However, often you will encounter this kind of exchange when you give someone positive feedback about their appearance, athletic ability, or intelligence.

"Well, really my sister is the beauty in the family."
"My friend Joe is the true athlete. I can't compare to him."
"Cousin Steve is the real genius."

This is classic behavior—rejecting positive feedback ("can't take a compliment") and discounting your strengths.

Do I have a strength if I sometimes make mistakes or don't always use my strength?

Again the answer is yes; it is still a strength you retain and can leverage. However, many people will discount their strengths by over-focusing on their imperfections.

Do I have a strength if I didn't have to "work" for it?

Sometimes you will hear someone respond to a compliment by saying, "Oh, I was born that way; it just comes easy to me." They often wonder if they should take credit for a strength if they didn't have to work hard to develop it. Yes, feel grateful for this "gift" and add it to your list of strengths.

Acknowledging Your Strengths

To build this more complete inventory of your strengths, utilize the following:

1. **Strength Clusters and Categories** The Social Style Model (Merrill and Reid) describes four types of leaders: Analytical, Driver, Amiable, Expressive. They also list typical strengths for each leader.
   Analytical:
   - Objectivity
   - Precision
   - Thoroughness, attention to detail
   - Systematic thinking
   - Professional approach
   - Willingness to explore alternatives
   - Tendency to encourage others to think carefully, be rational

   Driver:
   - Decisiveness
   - Toughness
   - Efficiency
   - Candidness
   - Results orientation

- Pragmatism
- Willingness to take risks
- Tendency to encourage others to decide and take actions

Amiable:
- Supportiveness
- Empathy
- Trustworthiness
- Loyalty
- Team orientation
- Concern for others' development
- Willingness to share recognition
- Tendency to encourage others to look for win-win solutions

Expressive:
- Creativity
- A sense of fun
- Enthusiasm
- Energy
- Focus on the vision
- Team spirit
- Willingness to try new things
- Tendency to encourage others to be the best, break new ground

The StrengthsFinder 2.0 Model (Tom Rath) will also introduce you to a wide variety of strengths. Explore which ones fit you. In addition, think about core values as strengths (e.g., empathy, respect, fairness, generosity, honesty, etc.).

2. **Analyze Success in Terms of Strengths** We have already explained the potential benefits to your career that accrue from analyzing your successes and achievements. Let's add one more. Your achievements also reveal your strengths. So ask that extra question, "What strengths did I leverage to achieve these results?"

3. **Your Network** Usually there are at least some people in your network who really "get" you." They understand your values and your intentions as well as your talents and potential. Learn to be receptive to their positive reflections, to be able to take in and savor a compliment.

Who knows, some day you may be able to channel Shonda Rhimes and say, "I totally deserve this positive feedback."

One final thought: If doing enough promotion is a challenge for you, here is another source of motivation. If you are representing your team in a meeting, on a call, or at a conference, you are their voice to convey their accomplishments, progress, and learning.

Paula's CEO Perspective

Over the course of 30 years of my career, I have seen it over and over. A female executive and I have a career conversation. She is always shy about her strengths and never outspoken about her wins in the business. For the most part, she is worried more about what she is missing than about what she brings to the table. She feels incomplete, as if she were forever a work in progress. Sometimes when you compliment her and recite one after the other all her wonderful strengths, something incredible happens: she gets emotional and begins to cry. (I always have tissues on hand.)

Nothing is more powerful than one woman telling another how incredible she is. (Do it often because it feels amazing!)

This "decent boldness" that Marty describes is not something that comes easily to women. It needs a high dose of rationalization for women to feel comfortable. What I have learned to say to women is to frame your boldness as pure, informative facts. Facts are facts and can't be discussed because they are mathematical. If you detail your strengths this way, it becomes easier to communicate (for example, reached target ahead of time, increased share, completed project on budget, consistently delivered results last five years, received highest internal survey results, and so on). Facts do help, but what women have to understand is that it's also your *internal ambition* that is so interesting for the organization. Women's ambitions are the best-kept secret in town. Nobody really knows what a professional woman aspires to do. It's her deepest secret. This "secret boldness" doesn't help you at all. It boils inside you and only creates frustration. Ambitions and strengths in women are a potent combination for success when women are vocal; they must be said out loud and to as many stakeholders as possible. Vocal ambitions and strengths create a fantastic "glow" in women. Organizations are often pleasantly surprised and very willing to accompany women on that growth path. So shake it off. Secrets are damaging. Speaking clearly about your strengths and squarely about your ambitions is the right way to go. Marty calls it decent boldness. I just call it the right thing to do.

.... LEADERSHIP PROFILE ....

Judith Atyaug Obari

Judith Atyaug Obari is the trust manager of the Akukuranut Development Trust and a member of the board of directors of Alupe Sub-County Hospital and World Neighbors Kenya. In all of her roles, she focuses on education, reproductive health, and HIV prevention. Her calling in life is to encourage women to overcome intimidation, stand up, and speak out. In recognition of all of her contributions, in 2018 she received the Best Person in Kenya award.

Judith remembers that when she was 10 years old, she "wanted to be somebody." She did well in school, but her education might have ended after primary school because of the fees required to continue. Fortunately one of her aunts came forward and sponsored her education. Judith made the most out of this opportunity. She worked hard, did well, and went on to the University of Nairobi and then postgraduate work at Busoga University in Uganda. When she was 26 she did an internship with a group that provided support to orphans, vulnerable children, AIDS patients, and sex workers. This became a key turning point in her life and put her on the path to encourage and empower women.

Judith has many qualities that make her so successful: intelligence, work ethic, an ability to build cohesive, effective teams, and a strong determination to leverage the strength of "sisterhood."

Two attributes make her a role model for many women. Judith is confident and bold. Even as a young woman, she was a leader of a team of men, almost all of them older than her—something very rare in Kenya at that time. Judith's life and impact provide a vivid example of the power of decent boldness.

Every day she strives to transfer this boldness to the women she works with on her projects. Judith often remarks that "women need to come up" and overcome intimidation. This includes standing up and speaking up together. "It is in the strength of sisterhood that women find their voice."

◆

Rule 8 Self-Assessment: Promote Yourself with Decent Boldness

Score yourself in these five areas, with 1 being "not at all," and 5 being "all the time."

1. I document my accomplishments and ideas to ensure proper recognition and credit.

    ①   ②   ③   ④   ⑤

2. I take advantage of exposure to top management to make appropriate references to my ideas, competence, results, and achievements.

    ①   ②   ③   ④   ⑤

3. I self-promote my capabilities and achievements with a balance of confidence and modesty.

    ①   ②   ③   ④   ⑤

4. I discuss my contributions in terms of learning that will help the organization, so that I do not come across as bragging.

    ①   ②   ③   ④   ⑤

5. I have prepared ways to describe my value-added contributions to the organization in a succinct, benefit-oriented way instead of just giving a job title.

    ①   ②   ③   ④   ⑤

Promote Yourself With Decent Boldness Action Plans

Use your low scores to guide you toward an action plan.

1. ....

....

2. ....

....

3. ....

....

CHAPTER 12

Rule 9: Enhance Your Executive Presence and Impact

We convince by our presence.
—Walt Whitman

A s you read previously, executive presence is a loosely defined concept mostly viewed from a male lens. In my experience, it is not evenly or fairly applied. So why create a rule for it? My insider position as an executive coach has allowed me to observe how often executive presence was a factor in who got promoted and who didn't. So we are going to pin down some specifics about this concept and give you a substantial number of tips to increase your presence and impact, and not allow these issues to detract from your leadership profile.

We will focus on:

- Gravitas
- Confident communication
- The impact of nonverbal behavior

But first I want to frame a key disadvantage many women have with regard to presence and impact. As we have seen, so often this disadvantage, ironically, springs from some superior qualities and good intentions women possess.

Journalists Katty Kay and Claire Shipman have reported on research indicating the following: Hard work and discipline help girls outperform boys in school, but that advantage disappears in the workforce. Girls are more disciplined regarding schoolwork, study harder, and consistently outperformed boys academically, and yet in the workplace 95 percent of the top positions are held by men. The key reason they found for this discrepancy is that men are far ahead of women when it comes to work-related confidence. "Underqualified and overprepared men don't think twice about leaning in. Overqualified and overprepared, too many women still hold back. Women feel confident only when they are perfect."

Another way of capturing this phenomenon is that men's threshold of certainty is lower than women's. So in an average meeting, women have a higher standard to meet before they will express their views confidently. This leave them vulnerable to several types of "self-censoring":

"How can I be sure?"

"What if I'm wrong?"

The net result is that some women may under-participate in discussions or make their points tentatively or softly, instantly detracting from their presence and impact (and of course also affecting levels of self-promotion). Rule 9 is going to give you some remedies for under-participation. It can't be good for any organization to have the less-prepared people doing the talking and the more knowledgeable people staying quiet.

Gravitas

Gravitas in Latin means "weight" or "heaviness." When someone is described as having gravitas, it means they convey a depth of thinking and a seriousness about their topic and a composure in their learning. If they smile or use humor, it is appropriate to their remarks. Some of the ways people inadvertently hurt their chances of being seen as possessing gravitas are smiling too much or at the wrong moments, using silly or self-deprecating humor, and appearing "scattered."

To improve your gravitas, learn how to be calm, centered and composed. There are many techniques to create a calm, centered core. I like breathing techniques because they yield quick results and you can use them anytime, anyplace. My favorite is the frozen rope technique.

The frozen rope is one of hundreds of breathing and concentration techniques that are used to quiet the mind and achieve tranquility. I prefer the frozen rope because it promotes the ability to concentrate as well as relax. People have long used breathing as a way to achieve inner control because it is both a voluntary and an involuntary process. If we choose, we can direct the rhythm of our breathing and influence some of our inner processes, including our level of relaxation and calm.

1. To begin the frozen rope, sit comfortably with your back straight; loosen any belts or clothing that would restrict your breathing.

2. Make your exhalations slow and even. Start by closing your eyes, breathing in deeply through your nose; then exhale slowly and smoothly through your mouth. As you exhale, imagine that your breath is extending like a frozen rope of air. Concentrate on the slow, even flow of air and the picture of the frozen rope.

3. At the end of the exhalation, wait a couple of seconds before you inhale. Initially, this will seem hard, so don't force it; later, as your breathing slows down, you will look forward to these very peaceful seconds, breathing neither in nor out but simply sitting quietly and concentrating on the frozen rope of air. When you inhale, allow your body to breathe as quickly and deeply as necessary to fill your lungs. Then begin the slow, even exhalation again.

Five to 10 minutes of this breathing and concentration will usually produce good results. An added benefit of the frozen rope exercise is that after you've done it regularly for a while, you can often trigger relaxation with only one to three breaths. Doing it 5 or 10 minutes a day is better than an hour one day a week. This type of breathing is a multiuse skill; once you become proficient, you can induce calm in almost any setting.

The consistent practice of some form of meditation has been demonstrated to yield the following benefits:

- Alleviates depression
- Stimulates parts of the brain associated with positive emotions
- Lowers blood pressure
- Speeds recovery from stress
- Increases concentration and the ability to stay fully engaged in the present moment

Additionally, for at least a few minutes a day, the meditator is receiving the internal message that simply "being" is a source of happiness. Notice the last benefit. This type of practice creates a state of "relaxed alertness." You are fully present, focused on the task at hand. Your conscious mind and intuition are picking up the key verbal and non-verbal clues you need to navigate a meeting. Participants sense that you are not carrying previous events with you or anticipating later appointments. You are completely present and they can feel it.

Develop Natural Conviction

You have probably heard the advice "Fake it until you make it." It kind of reminds me of the Groucho Marx joke, "Sincerity is the most cherished virtue. If you can fake that, you can accomplish anything." I guess it can help in some circumstances, but I recommend building gravitas on a more solid foundation: natural conviction. We all know people who you could literally wake from a deep sleep, mention a topic, and they can expound on it confidently. If you are not this way, you need to prepare to the point that you have conviction and passion about your subject. A very useful saying to point you in this direction is, "The most important sale you will ever make is to sell yourself first." Another way to remember to do this is to spell the word *enthusIASM*: I Am Sold Myself. If you go to presentations or meetings with conviction and passion for what you are saying, it will dramatically increase your gravitas and your impact.

Confident Communication

High-impact communicators are crisp and focused. They adjust their remarks to the needs and level of the audience. They are usually effective at making clear the "so what" of their presentation and creating urgency for their recommendations. At meetings you can increase your executive presence and impact with the following executive vocabulary.

Use language of conviction, with phrases such as:

- *"My point of view . . ."*
- *"I recommend . . ."*
- *"I suggest . . ."*
- *"Based on our experience . . ."*
- *"My advice would be . . ."*
- *"If it were my decision, I would . . ."*

Use language for challenging others, with phrases such as:

- *"An issue we may face . . ."*
- *"As we go forward, I would pay attention to . . ."*
- *"Considering . . ."*
- *"In the implementation phase, I'd like us to stay focused on . . ."*
- *"A concern we may need to address . . ."*
- *"A challenge . . ."*
- *"How would we respond to . . ."*
- *"I'm not as confident . . ."*
- *"I'm not convinced this will get us to where we need to be."*

The language of conviction allows you to make your perspective clear while avoiding phrases that might seem arrogant or pushy such as

- *"We have to . . ."*
- *"This is the only way to go . . ."*
- *"It's a no-brainer . . ."*

The language for challenging others helps you on many levels. You earn a very desirable reputation as someone who says what needs to be said, is not shy about challenging others or surfacing conflict, but is always respectful. These phrases give you some basic starting points. You can add your own style and approach and adjust to the circumstances. For example: "Joe, I see why you are excited about this new process, and the potential upside versus the way we are doing it now is clear. Here's my remaining concern. I've listened carefully but I haven't heard an answer to . . ."

Focusing on the Real Risk

One way to overcome the kind of self-censoring that inhibits or softens participation is to take a hard look at the risks at a meeting or on a conference call:

- Risk of making someone angry
- Risk of saying something stupid
- Risk of underparticipating/low impact

What is the risk that you will say something that makes someone angry to the point it hurts your career? I would say for most of you this is very low. For starters, many readers of this book are on the polite, respectful, tactful side, and now you have the benefit of executive vocabulary to calibrate your message. Some people may not be happy about the information you are inserting into the discussion, but you are conveying it respectfully and are entitled to have a different perspective.

What is the risk that you will say something so stupid that people will think, "I always thought Rebecca was smart but now I'm not so sure"? Again, very low. Remember Kay and Shipman's findings. You are likely to be thorough and prepared and very unlikely to say something in a careless and sloppy way. In any case, we all have been in meetings where people said questionable things without repercussions. Putting this all together, the career risk of a "stupid" remark on your part is low.

What is the career risk if you go to meeting after meeting where the discussions center on areas about which you are knowledgeable and experienced and you are quiet, under-participate, or contribute in a tentative manner? VERY HIGH. You would likely be hurting yourself in terms of self-promotion, strategic thinking, and thought leadership, as well as executive presence and impact. So please, if I've convinced you, before your next meeting or conference, remind yourself, "My greatest risk at this moment is under-participating. People need to know I was here!"

The Impact of Nonverbal Behavior

Research does show that if the nonverbal component of your communication conveys confidence and presence you are much more likely to persuade and influence. So steady eye contact, a firm handshake, strong voice, and an erect posture with a wide stance (feet shoulder-width apart) all contribute mightily. In addition to working on these behaviors, it's crucial to eliminate any detractors. I'll just list the actions to watch out for discussed previously.

Please get feedback from people you trust about the following:

- Being too polite

- Over-smiling or smiling at the wrong time
- Being deferential
- Seeking too much approval
- Over-apologizing
- Using self-deprecating statements or humor
- Using a soft voice
- Using too many qualifiers and tentative statements

  "I haven't totally thought this through but . . ."

  "This is kind of outside my area of expertise but . . ."

  "Would it sound silly to . . ."

- Shying away from public conflict
- Allowing oneself to be marginalized in a meeting

Paula's CEO Perspective

I agree with Marty that the list above typically derails women in the work environment. So many times I have had to interrupt a talented female executive to say, "*I can't hear you. Can you speak louder, please?*" Or I have shushed a loud group in the meeting room for a soft female executive voice only to hear her say the most important comment of the entire day and have the crowd nodding in agreement. But there are also a group of us who are outliers. We speak loudly and make our voices heard. We are direct, assertive, the opposite of tentative. We almost never smile or are overpolite. We don't shy away from conflict; in fact, sometimes we even prefer it. Unfortunately, this, too, is a problem. Other authors call this the "likability double-bind." A Catch-22 of women leadership. If you happen to be on my team, I have two pieces of advice:

1. Authenticity is important. At the end of the day we are who we are, and this is not about changing yourself into something different. What is useful, however, is to be a *centered* authentic version of yourself.

2. Being centered for the outliers like me can be difficult. Marty recommends breathing. I recommend one phrase from my yoga instructor. I started yoga after Marty suggested it for

breathing exercises. I didn't learn breathing techniques, but I learned to "align my components." My yoga instructor constantly repeats "align your components," meaning you align your shoulder, elbow, wrist or align your foot, knee, hip. In business situations, I repeat to myself, "align your components," meaning all the different angles in your personality that are so wonderful when they are completely centered and synchronized. Marty calls it self-talk. I have to constantly "align my components" to be 100 percent more effective in anything I do.

-------------------------------- LEADERSHIP PROFILE --------------------------------

Ofra Strauss

"With power and success comes responsibility," shared Ofra Strauss. As chairperson of the Strauss Group, a global food company based in Israel, Ofra has dedicated her life to more than just advancing and developing the company. From CEO at age 35 to chairperson at 40, she's invested her time and work ethic to empower and help women make a difference.

Ofra's mother was a Holocaust survivor who had escaped from Croatia to Italy, then to Switzerland, and finally to Israel. Her father's parents left Nazi Germany in 1936, setting foot in what would later become Israel. The family business was established not long after their arrival, with two cows on a small vegetable farm in the remote town of Nahariya.

Ofra proudly remembers her father describing her mother as the bravest woman he'd ever met. She says she was lucky enough to have had, both in her formative years and early in her career, female role models who were hard workers and equal contributors.

Women were pivotal in making the family business thrive. At the young age of 11, Ofra joined her father on delivery routes where, in addition to carrying 20-kilogram containers of dairy products, she learned the basic elements of what made the business tick: hard work and relationships with people.

"Work brought me honor," she explains. "I was brought up in a family where work was a value because it meant you could provide for your family." From two cows in 1937, the family business grew to become the second largest food-products manufacturer in Israel and an international company. For over 20 years, PepsiCo has been partnering with Strauss: from salty snacks in Israel to the Sabra-Obela hummus and dips Joint Venture, the largest hummus manufacturer worldwide.

Ofra became chairperson of Strauss Group in 2001, inheriting the great responsibility for the family and business legacy and high expectations for the future. Soon after, she was asked how it felt to be the only woman in a position of such high rank. That question, which came up again and again, brought her to the realization that having so few women in business leadership positions is a problem, and it relates to wider societal gender disparities. From that moment on, she took it upon herself to raise the flag for women's empowerment.

At the beginning of her journey to empower women, Ofra joined an NGO to help fundraising for shelters for domestic abuse victims. Later, she led the Catalyst Census's launch in Israel, to promote public discourse on women's representation in Israel's top one hundred public companies.

In 2012, Ofra helped to establish Jasmine, an NGO promoting Jewish and Arab Israeli women's entrepreneurship. Jasmine became a community of women who work hard to help each other build businesses and remove the obstacles they face in becoming successful business owners. Bringing together Jewish and Arab women, Jasmine promotes the empowerment of women in the business realm, as well as encourages dialogue and mutual understanding, thus promoting peace.

In its first seven years of operation, Jasmine helped more than 12,000 women with economic development, empowerment, personal tutoring for their businesses, business management training, technology training, and even a social business program. This changes the reality not only of the women taking part in the NGO's programs but also the reality of the families, their communities, and the state of Israel.

A champion of equality, inclusiveness, and peace, Ofra Strauss is a woman who empowers other women, and those women then work to empower more women. She continues to show up with her notebook, ready to learn from the women around her. With more than 30 years on her women's empowerment journey, she embraces the community of women she meets with eagerness. Ofra is breaking barriers and using her power to effect a positive change in the world.

◆

Rule 9 Self-Assessment: Enhance Your Executive Presence and Impact

Score yourself in these five areas, with 1 being "not at all," and 5 being "all the time."

1. I project an aura of confidence through my appearance, body language, voice, and vocabulary.

   ①   ②   ③   ④   ⑤

2. I optimize my impact at meetings by actively contributing, speaking with conviction, and protecting my "airtime."

   ①   ②   ③   ④   ⑤

3. I know when to present my ideas more forcefully and when to be more invitational in order to take into account ego and power dynamics.

   ①   ②   ③   ④   ⑤

4. When discussing serious, meaningful issues, my demeanor conveys gravitas.

   ①   ②   ③   ④   ⑤

5. I check in with trusted members of my network to get feedback about my executive presence and impact.

   ①   ②   ③   ④   ⑤

Enhance Your Executive Presence and Impact Action Plans

Use your low scores to guide you toward an action plan.

1. ....

   ....

2. ....

   ....

3. ....

   ....

CHAPTER 13

Rule 10:
Protect Yourself from
Sabotage and Marginalization

Before we provide tips and strategies to protect yourself, let's look at specific examples of how these actions look in the workplace. Let's start with the ones you have already read about:

Anne/Stuart, pages 47-50: We saw that Stuart combined sabotage and marginalization. He misinformed Anne, telling her that she did not need to be at certain meetings, then used her absence of knowledge to put her at a disadvantage with her boss. He used his access to Charles to "manage the airwaves" against Anne by creating the buzz that would hurt the most with Charles: She "doesn't like to get her hands dirty" likes to "operate at 30,000 feet."

Marty/David, pages 77-78: David tried to make me radioactive with my clients by using the words *investigate, money,* and *fixit program,* and by twisting a request from the head of HR for his own purposes.

Amy/Sam, pages 93-96: Despite rejecting Amy's idea twice, Sam took full credit for the value strategy and promoted it throughout the company.

Another example you read about on page 60 is someone going to a leader who values strategic thinking as the top leadership skill, describing me in terms of "point him in the right direction" and "you have to call the plays for him."

There are many other examples of sabotage and marginalizing actions, big and small:

- Not providing timely information
- Providing misleading information

- Getting you upset before a meeting or presentation or making you late for a meeting
- Someone blaming you for their mistakes
- Agreeing to present results of a project together and then giving the information by themselves
- Not keeping information confidential
- Interrupting you in meetings so you don't finish your thought or changing the subject after you have made a point that is important to you
- Squeezing your time at a presentation or even taking it out entirely
- And with new technology, I'm sure there are many other ways to sabotage people that I'm not even aware of!

Protecting Yourself

When I introduced the rules, I mentioned that each rule had a proactive value and a protective value, so if you have been practicing previous rules, you are actually well on your way to protecting yourself. Practicing "Detect to Protect," you are now able to identify and therefore predict who is most likely to engage in these behaviors. Some specific tips to help you deal with these types of people:

Document. It's very important to document discussions, what was agreed to in meetings, who did the work, and so on. Also note if there was abusive or inappropriate behavior.

Get there early. Remember, a key tactic is "managing the airwaves." So get there before them, or as early as possible. For example, an overly political person with a hidden personal agenda wants you to commit to a certain project. To you, this project doesn't advance the company's objectives, and so you don't go along with his request. He is likely to go to your bosses and say that you are rigid, inflexible, unwilling to try new things, or not a team player. You get there early and say, "Joe and I had a good discussion about his new proposal. We tried to come up with a win-win but couldn't, so for now we are going to agree to disagree. I'm not convinced this is going to achieve our objectives."

Use power, play hardball. Remember that Power Over people are studying you. If they think you are reluctant to use your power, they will be not afraid to treat you in a shabby way.

If there are situations where demoting or firing someone is the right thing to do for your team or the organization, it is important for others to see you don't shy away from those decisions.

Know your buzz. Now we see even more why each of us needs to stay current about our buzz. If someone is trying to hurt our reputation, we need to learn about it as soon as possible.

It is also useful to anticipate how someone will go after you. Anne, for example, could have anticipated that someone would say she didn't have industry knowledge.

What could someone say about you that might stick, if they wanted to create a negative buzz?

Leverage your network. This is probably the best way to protect yourself. A strong, active network will inform you about someone trying to take credit for your work or ideas, assign blame, or badmouth you. These people will have your back. If you use your network to be your eyes and ears, you will gain a very useful reputation as someone who "sees it coming."

Increase your value to the organization. The more other people see you as valued by senior management, the less likely negative buzz will stick to you.

Promote yourself with decent boldness. Putting your handprint on your work, branding your projects and ideas, and discussing your results in terms of organizational learning with a wide audience will act as a shield if someone tries to take credit for your work.

Enhance your executive presence. Your gravitas, forcefulness, and ease with challenge, debate, and conflict send a message that you are someone who will defend yourself skillfully.

So the good news is that you are well on your way to having the skills to deal with these attempts. But the best news is that by internalizing the rules you actually reduce the chances that people will go after you. You take the target off your back.

Additional Verbal Skills

Marginalization often comes in small ways. Someone interrupting you or changing the subject or shrinking your time are little ways of taking away your seat at the table.

Sometimes people will tease you or be sarcastic, and then if you respond, they will say you are too sensitive. So it's important to have the verbal responses ready for these actions. They can not only block the marginalizing behavior, they can actually enhance your image as someone who will make sure she is respected and treated fairly.

Before I describe some of this language, I want to encourage you to also learn from other people in your organization or the public arena who do this well.

A recent public example is: In December 2018, at a televised meeting of President Donald Trump, Democratic Senate leader Chuck Schumer, and House Speaker Nancy Pelosi, President Trump started to say, "Well, Nancy doesn't feel strongly about . . ." Speaker Pelosi quickly interrupted the president and said, "Don't characterize how I feel, and please do not speak for me." Now it takes practice and experience to be as quick and sharp as Speaker Pelosi or Ambassador Haley, but we can all get better at responding to someone trying to marginalize our power.

Interrupting. Meetings are fast paced and interruptions are common. But if an interruption substantially disrupts you communicating a message that is important, it needs to be addressed. "Let me finish my point" or "Okay, finish your thought, but then I want to get back to my point." You definitely need to be ready. A 2014 George Washington University study found that men interrupt women 33 percent more than they interrupt other men. This pattern has even gotten the attention of the US Court system. It has decided to intervene after finding that female judges and attorneys were regularly interrupted by their male counterparts. Then I guess it is no surprise that the most interrupted Supreme Court Justice is Justice Sonia Sotomayor.

Diverting. A subtle form of marginalizing is when another person jumps in right after you make an important point and then changes the subject. You are left there dangling with no response to something that mattered to you. If you don't say anything, this will keep happening. "Before we go on to that topic, I would like to get some feedback on what I just suggested." "Let's get closure on this topic before we move on." Or "I know that topic is important to you, but what I just said is important to me too. I'd like to get some responses to my suggestion before we move on."

Taking your time away. If one of your peers comes to you and says, "Caroline, I know you were scheduled to present today, but the agenda is really crowded, and we need to resolve the budget issue by Friday. I think we should postpone your piece until next month."

You might reply, "Actually, there are several crucial messages I will be presenting. I'll explain the urgency to our boss, and then he can decide what he wants to keep on the agenda."

Teasing/sarcasm directed at you. This is a very clever form of marginalization. If you don't say anything, the negative messages may linger and even stick to you. If you get defensive, your adversary is likely to say you are "thin-skinned," "too sensitive" "overreacting," or "emotional." An effective way to respond is "Joe, I know you are just joking, but since you have brought up that issue, I'd like to address it." Then, calmly give the group correct information about the issue Joe is teasing you about.

As with any skill, practice as much as you can. You can start in small, low-risk situations. We can't expect that people will agree with us or find our ideas fascinating, but we do have a right to be listened to and we do have a right to have a voice in discussions.

················· LEADERSHIP PROFILE ·················

Liezl Tolentino

Liezl is the top human resources executive at Enlivant. Enlivant operates over 230 senior living communities that comprise over 11,000 apartment units. Liezl and her team have been at the forefront of forging policies and processes to keep Enlivant's residents and employees healthy during the pandemic. Considering they are protecting the highest-risk population, their safety numbers have been truly outstanding.

Through it all, Enlivant has continued (for three straight years) to receive awards as a Great Place to Work. At work, Liezl is a mentor to many women, and her external activities focus on creating educational opportunities for young women.

Liezl's parents are from the Philippines, and they both came from large families (dad one of 10, mom one of 8). She credits many of her core values and key skills to her home environment. At an early age she learned to build relationships with a wide variety of people. She internalized the value of helping others and sharing success. And even before Jack Welch coined the term, Liezl experienced the benefits of living in a "feedback-rich" environment. In that way, her family members taught her to be coachable, transparent, and accountable. All these qualities make Liezl a Power With leader who excels at collaboration.

None of these strengths, though, have prevented her from experiencing attempts at marginalizing, gaslighting, or undermining her credibility. As her career progressed, she often found herself as the only woman on a team.

She has been able to meet these challenges and protect herself in the following ways:

- Relying on the resilience and mental toughness she developed in her childhood
- At times directly confronting other people's comments and/or narratives
- Leveraging her network

Liezl is a big believer that no one can sustain a career trajectory alone; there are too many landmines and ways to get off track. She credits her network for at times giving her a heads-up about attempts to tarnish her standing, and at other times jumping in to support her.

◆

Rule 10 Self-Assessment: Protect Yourself from Sabotage and Marginalization

Score yourself in these five areas, with 1 being "not at all," and 5 being "all the time."

1. Instead of being overly trusting, I anticipate and expect sabotage and influence challenges as possible.

    (1)   (2)   (3)   (4)   (5)

2. I use networking relationships to discover and protect against power plays or undermining efforts.

    (1)   (2)   (3)   (4)   (5)

3. When being badmouthed or attacked behind the scenes, I form a plan to reduce any negative impact.

    (1)   (2)   (3)   (4)   (5)

4. I respond nondefensively yet firmly to public put-downs, sarcasm, or insults.

    (1)   (2)   (3)   (4)   (5)

5. Before counterattacking a saboteur, I make sure it's necessary, assess the possible consequences, and rally powerful supporters.

    (1)   (2)   (3)   (4)   (5)

Protect Yourself from Sabotage and Marginalization Action Plans

Use your low scores to guide you toward an action plan.

1. ....

2. ....

3. ....

CHAPTER 14

Rule 11:
Develop Healthy Selfishness

Healthy selfishness is a desire for success and happiness built on a foundation of:

Self-valuing

Self-acceptance

Self-care

When I introduced this concept I mentioned a study that showed women too often over-volunteering for less visible projects and then underpromoting those activities. Men were more likely to selectively commit to activities that were on the senior management's "scorecard" and to make sure the organization knew about their efforts.

Without the attitudes and skills of healthy selfishness, there is a real risk of overcommitting, over-self-reliance, and putting oneself at a distinct disadvantage. As is our practice, let's review a case study where the lack of these skills, despite good intentions, threatened to undermine a woman's career momentum.

> Deborah was raised in the US Midwest, the youngest of four siblings (three older brothers). Her family emphasized a strong work ethic, self-reliance, and making do with the resources they had. Her female role models in the family all seemed to put other people's needs ahead of their own. As far back as she could remember, Deborah had a deep interest in and fascination with television.
>
> After graduating from university, she moved to New York City and joined the FunTime Network, which is composed of three cable channels that offer a variety of children's programs. She is now 39

years old, married, and with 11-year-old twin girls who are entering middle school. Her parents are now in their late 70s, and while they still live in their home, they have some health issues that need monitoring. Her brothers have said they would provide financial support if necessary but clearly expect that Deborah will be the guardian of the health-care decisions.

After 10 successful years at the FunTime channel that targeted the preadolescent audience, Deborah has been promoted to president of the FunTime Jr. channel (a four-to six-year-old audience).

In her first 60 days in the new role, the following events occurred:

- The CEO of FunTime took her to lunch and discussed the FunTime Jr. team. He mentioned that the head of programming was a marginal performer. Although he said he would understand it if Deborah wanted to replace him, he was hoping she might be able to salvage him. She said she would try.

- The head of operations approached Deborah about co-chairing the company's new "Green Initiative" task force. He said it was an important priority for the company to look at practices that promoted a sustainable environment and healthier buildings for FunTime employees. She agreed to co-chair the task force.

- The woman who provided childcare for Deborah and her husband was in an automobile accident and her recovery time was expected to be six weeks. Deborah did not have a backup, and she and her husband were splitting time doing work at home after their daughters got home from school.

- Given her new responsibilities and the childcare challenges, Deborah has decided to take a two-month break from her twice weekly Pilates class.

For leaders at Deborah's level, FunTime uses a new leader assimilation program called the First 90 Days. After 60 days in the role, human resources conducts a series of interviews at all levels of the organization to gather perspectives about Deborah's leadership. The interviews revealed the following feedback:

- Her senior team voiced frustrations at not always being able to obtain her guidance or have her make timely decisions.

- Several people mentioned that Deborah often joked or made side comments about how busy she was.
- At a recent meeting of the FunTime Network senior team, Deborah arrived late and the materials she used in her presentation were not effectively organized.

This feedback was given to Deborah as well as the CEO. His initial reaction was, "I wonder if she is in over her head."

Case Study Questions and Analysis

Is Deborah being realistic about her current commitments and responsibilities? Why?

How is Deborah lacking in "healthy selfishness"? How is it hurting her? What should she do now?

What can we learn from Deborah's mistakes?

1. **Be realistic about what's on your plate.** It's important to be realistic about what commitments you already have. Deborah had childcare and eldercare responsibilities in addition to this big promotion.

2. **Don't just "make do."** Given Deborah's responsibilities, she really cannot afford to make do with a marginal performer. She should act more in her self-interest and replace this marginal performer while she has a window to do it.

3. **Don't be a hero.** Given the reality of her situation, is this the right time to co-chair the new task force? No. This is a perfect example of a worthy initiative that she should say no to. (In Rule 12 we will introduce the concept of the soft no, which Deborah could use to respond to this request.)

4. **Maintain your exercise routine.** This is a time when Deborah needs her Pilates class or some form of exercise more than ever. Exercise is what gives you the mental clarity and stamina to deal with a busy schedule.

5. **Pay enough attention to optics, perception, and buzz.** Deborah is creating negative impressions with a group that does not know her that well.

So Deborah's situation is a classic example of why we need healthy selfishness attitudes and skills. Her intentions were good regarding the marginal performer, Green Initiative, and sacrificing her Pilates class, but these actions undermined her chances of success.

The Foundations of Healthy Selfishness

Self-Valuing

- "I'm not more important than anyone else, but my time, energy, plans/priorities, and personal power are important to me. I am going to act to preserve them."
- "I minimize thoughts and emotions that waste time and energy, distract me, or give away my power."
- "I have the skills to effectively deal with people who try to divert me or marginalize me."
- "I think carefully about what I say yes to, and I'm comfortable saying no."

Self-Acceptance

"I accept that I am a fallible human being. I have blind spots, skill deficits, and knowledge gaps. That is why I accept and seek feedback and don't expect to be perfect. I don't waste time and energy beating myself up about mistakes. I put my focus on what I can improve and what I can learn. My power comes from my belief that I can grow and change. This allows me to calmly review or critique my performance without being harsh to myself."

Self-Care

If someone offered you career success, but the costs would be that your health would deteriorate, you would lose your integrity, and you would be estranged from your friends and family, I doubt that you would make these tradeoffs. Yet because harm to our health, values, and relationships happens so gradually, many people are actually making these precious tradeoffs every day. One hundred and fifty years ago, Dostoevsky said, "If people lost their souls overnight, they would notice and be desperate to get them back. But people lose their souls so gradually they don't notice until it is too late." So people don't make the conscious decision, "I am not going to take care of myself," but the net result is the same as if they did.

In Deborah's case, we can see that self-care is actually a necessary part of keeping your career on a positive path. Self-care includes:

- Adequate sleep
- Decent nutrition
- Exercise
- Time to maintain key personal relationships
- Time for rest/recovery

In addition to these basic self-care activities, we encourage you to integrate the following into your day:

Breaks. Most of us were not taking many breaks when we were going into the office every day. Since the COVID-19 epidemic began, with many of us confined to home, breaks have continued to disappear. Back-to-back Zoom calls and meetings and interruptions from your personal life add to stress and reduce our effectiveness in the short and long term. Even just starting a new meeting when you are stressed or distracted from one that just ended is not setting yourself up for success. Here are some recommended breaks, even if they are only 5 minutes:

Movement

Stretching

A few minutes of fresh air or nature

Slow, focused breathing

Gratitude

Music

Reflection

Slow, Focused Breathing

As part of the skill of calm self-critique, you were introduced to the practice of slow, focused breathing. In terms of self-care and improving your impact and effectiveness, few activities convey as many benefits in such a short amount of time. Learning to quickly become calm and centered has payoffs for:

Starting your day

Improving your executive presence

Rebalancing after an upsetting or frustrating meeting so that it doesn't carry over to the next one

Gratitude

"Too blessed to be stressed." Research in neuroscience over the last 10 years has confirmed the wisdom of this saying. Our brain patterns show that gratitude lights up our "happiness" centers and immediately reduces our stress.

Gratitude is the state of being thankful and appreciative. I am fortunate to have learned about the healing and energizing power of gratitude relatively early in my life. When I was 20, I entered a monastery in Kyoto, Japan. The day-to-day living conditions fell somewhere between minimal and harsh: We had no beds, heat, or showers. Food was not plentiful, and my weight dropped from 198 to 138 pounds in a year. Despite the lack of many comforts, it was the most important and, in many ways, the happiest year of my life. Several monastery practices sustained me, and one of those was the practice of being grateful. It was built into every facet of the day. We stopped to be grateful many times a day, and were taught to be thankful to our parents, teachers, and the farmers who grew the food we ate. So even in the absence of many basic necessities or common comforts, I learned to appreciate, to be grateful for, what I had.

Thus, the essence of gratitude is focus. Focusing on what you don't have, on what others possess that you don't, may be useful for goal setting, but it will not send you (or your nervous system) the positive messages and wonderful sensation that gratitude can deliver. Almost any system or religion you embrace would accept that simply being human is a miracle and a gift. Our basic senses' and rational minds' capacity for feeling and creating bonds with people are gifts we sometimes take for granted until they are impaired or threatened.

Cultivating gratitude is one of the most effective stress management (not to mention happiness) practices there is, providing tranquility and a balanced perspective. Many people, including myself, find that an excellent way to start every day is to focus on what you are grateful for. Say thank you for being alive, for your health, and the health of those close to you, for your strengths and resources; extend your thanks to other people or a higher power. Leave no stone unturned in being grateful. Commuting to work, enhance your optimism and energy by focusing on what you like about, and are grateful for, at your job. For example, my work consists of writing, coaching, or teaching seminars. Before I begin any of these tasks, I take two minutes to remind myself how fortunate I am to have each opportunity to present my ideas and, possibly, have a positive impact on someone's life. A simple but effective gratitude exercise for the end of the day is to think about at least three good things that happened to you during that day. Then, to add to your learning (and for a change of pace), analyze how and why they happened.

Gratitude is a skill you can develop through repetition and practice. Like all the skills in this section, it is a blend of what we choose to focus on and what we say to ourselves. It is a basic building block of an effective stress management plan.

The Power of Self-Talk

There is a person with whom you spend more time with than any other, a person who has more influence over your growth than anyone else. This ever-present companion is your own self. This self guides you, belittles you, or supports you.

You engage this person in an ever-constant dialogue—a dialogue through which you set goals for yourself, make decisions, feel pleased, dejected, or despondent. In short, your behavior, feelings, sense of self-esteem, and even level of stress are influenced by your inner speech.

—Pamela Butler, *Talking to Yourself* (HarperCollins, 1991)

This inner speech is self-talk. Self-talk skills, including the ability to direct your focus and what you say to yourself, are an essential building block of any stress management plan. How you perceive events and circumstances, how you interpret the actions of others, and how you respond to situations in general all affect your stress level. In other words, your self-talk and your focus influence your level of stress whether you are aware of it or not. There are many techniques you can use to help you take charge of your self-talk and make it work for you.

A humorous way to see how our usual self-talk impacts our feelings and progress is to imagine a one-year-old baby's self-talk while learning how to walk.

Are You More Resilient Than a One-Year-Old?

In facing setbacks or severe challenges, resilient people have attitudes and skills that allow them to regain their confidence, composure, and concentration. In addition to taking positive, proactive actions, their main advantage is that they have learned what *not* to do in these situations.

An easy way to examine both sides of resilience is to think of a one-year-old trying to walk. When babies are on the cusp of walking, very motivated but not yet fully coordinated, they might fall down 25 times in a day. But each time they fall, they do five wonderful things:

- Stay focused on the goal: walking
- Pick themselves up
- Try again
- Get stronger muscles by pushing off the floor
- Learn about movement and balance

Even better than these five great practices is what they avoid doing after 25 "setbacks." Imagine what might go on in the mind of an average adult who was given a task at work and got it wrong 25 times in a day. Now imagine what would happen to a baby if he or she had some of our adult "self-talk" after we make repeated mistakes.

- "I can't believe it. I fell down 25 times today."
- "I'm such a klutz. I suck at walking."
- "My cousin Allison is only 11 months old and she is walking already. What's wrong with me?"
- "My first birthday party is next week. What if I fall down in front of my friends and family? I'll be humiliated."
- "I'll never learn how to walk."
- "If my mother would ever get me the right shoes and some diapers that fit, I'd be walking already."

These self-talk patterns don't lead to confidence, composure, and concentration. They wouldn't help a baby learn to walk, and they don't help us meet our challenges.

So ask yourself, what can you learn from a baby's approach to walking?

Can you identify any self-talk patterns that detract from your resilience, such as:

- Counting your mistakes
- Calling yourself names
- Unfavorably comparing yourself to others
- Catastrophizing about imagined future failures
- Giving up
- Blaming others

Self-Talk for Worry

"My life has been a series of terrible misfortunes . . . most of which never happened," said Mark Twain. "Cowards die many times before their deaths. The valiant never taste of death but once," wrote Shakespeare in *Julius Caesar*. These quotes illuminate the more significant and pervasive aspects of fear and worry: when we worry, we picture in great detail what we *perceive* as a horrible event or situation, and our nervous system reacts as if it is happening. Worrying, most often, is simply a form of "dread rehearsal." And the downsides are considerable. Worry narrows our focus, depletes energy, and wastes time; and it prompts our bodies to secrete high levels of stress hormones.

Clearly, it is more productive to use positive self-talk and focus skills than to spend time engaged in unproductive worrying. A good motto here is, "Improvement not perfection," because you won't be able to eliminate all anxiety no matter how diligent you are. Nevertheless, you can make great strides. As a starting point, learn to ask yourself the key questions I provide here to begin to help you worry less often and for shorter periods, and to reduce your level of anxiety.

Key Questions

1. *Am I worrying or planning?* Worrying can deplete your time and energy, and reduce your effectiveness. If you find yourself feeling anxious, ask yourself, "Am I worrying or planning?" Don't get bogged down in worry; instead, use it as a signal to anticipate, prevent, prepare, or plan more diligently.

2. *Is what I am worrying about a small possibility or a probability?* Mathematicians have shown that, from a straight probability perspective, most of us often worry about the wrong things. We fear events that are publicized, even though they may have a very low probability of occurring (contracting AIDS, being the victim of terrorism). At the same time,

we disregard actual dangerous situations—such as talking on a cell phone, applying makeup, eating, or even reading while driving 60 miles an hour on a busy freeway. So when you find yourself worrying, ask yourself, what is the actual possibility of this happening?

3. *If what I'm worrying about does happen, will it really be a catastrophe—or just an inconvenience?* This is probably the most important distinction to make to reduce your level of stress. Most of the things we worry about in our professional and personal lives do not fall in the catastrophe category. They are more accurately labeled inconveniences. True catastrophes are events like the genocide in Rwanda, 9/11, Hurricane Katrina, or serious health problems for you or your loved ones. Making a mistake during a presentation, missing a deadline, missing market-share benchmarks during a new product launch, getting passed over for a promotion, or even losing a job are not true catastrophes. They are setbacks, disappointments, losses, and, in some cases, major inconveniences, but they are not catastrophes.

   To help modify your way of thinking about such setbacks, ask, what is the worst that could happen? Let's say you get fired or your job is downsized. What would you do? First, consider all the other setbacks, problems, and obstacles you've overcome in your life. Second, consider viewing this as an opportunity to focus on your own development: you could gather feedback about your behavior or skills or try to figure out how to prevent this from happening in the future. Third, explore the possibility that this may be an opportunity to go down a different path, take a different role, join a different sort of company or industry, or maybe start up your own business. There are many examples of people who went on to achieve great things after being laid off by a company, and in retrospect were glad it happened. Think about it: it is highly likely you will find another job and highly unlikely you and your family will be out on the street. Your lifestyle may come down a notch or two, some luxuries may have to go, but *this is not a catastrophe.*

In summary, fear and worry don't help your performance. Preparation, planning, and giving your best effort do. Gathering feedback and learning from your mistakes do. When Eli Manning is throwing a football in the Super Bowl or Venus Williams is hitting a tennis ball at Wimbledon, fear and tension don't help. Practice and training, followed by focus and execution, do. It is possible to have high motivation and exert full effort to achieve your goals and still see things from a balanced perspective. In fact, it can help your confidence and composure when you realize your self-worth is not on the line for each project or performance.

Additional Useful Self-Talk for Worry

The following phrases, if you say them to yourself in the appropriate situations, can greatly reduce fear reactions. If you practice using them regularly, over time you will develop new, more useful mental habits.

1. "I focus on creating positive results in any situation. Problems give me an opportunity to learn and use my skills."

2. "I'm disappointed with the results I'm getting so far. I'd better find out as much as I can about what is going wrong in this situation so I can improve it or at least get feedback to help me perform better in the future."

3. "Stop! Fear and worrying are a waste of my time and energy and they block me from using my skills."

4. "I trust myself to acquire the knowledge and skills I need if this plan or approach does not lead to the results I want."

5. "I'm resourceful and I have the ability to bounce back. My trend is not my destiny because I can learn from my results and then change and adapt."

6. "My objectives in this situation are important. If I don't achieve them, I'll be disappointed and it will be inconvenient, but it will not be a catastrophe or a horrible event. By thinking about negative results as a catastrophe, I'm creating tension and fear that actually reduce my chance of success."

7. "I create pressure in any situation by what I focus on and what I say to myself. I can remove pressure by concentrating on doing the best job right now and learning all I can."

Self-Talk for Anger

Anger can be a useful emotion, indicating to yourself and others what is deeply important to you. It also can be used as a way to say to others that you won't be mistreated or taken advantage of. Anger may also serve as a springboard to discuss issues and concerns so that disagreements aren't allowed to fester and lead to long-term resentments. And, needless to say, anger can be a source of physical strength when we are faced with threats or challenges. That's the plus side of this emotion. On the other side is the obvious damage: too much anger, expressed in the wrong situations, can cause damage to our health, equilibrium, and relationships.

As Dr. Meyer Friedman and Ray Rosenman explain in *Type A Behavior and Your Heart,* anger results in a massive physiological preparation for action:

> If you become intensely angered by some phenomenon, your hypothalamus will almost instantaneously send signals to all or almost all the nerve endings of your sympathetic nervous system (that portion of your nervous system not directly under your control), causing them to secrete relatively large amounts of epinephrine and norepinephrine . . . In addition this same fit of anger will probably also induce the hypothalamus to send additional messages to the pituitary gland, the master of all endocrine glands, urging it to discharge some of its own exclusively manufactured hormones (such as growth hormone) and also to send out chemical signals to the adrenal, sex, and thyroid glands and the pancreas as well, so that they in turn may secrete excess amounts of their exclusively manufactured hormones.

Paula's CEO Perspective

Watch out for the wrong self-talk. It is vicious and damaging. Unfortunately, women go through life with an invisible sticker on their forehead that carries a self-directed debilitating message. As women leaders, we must be very active in peeling off this vicious self-talk from the foreheads of as many women as we can. It is totally liberating when one woman tells another the deep truth: the sticker you created is not true. You made up a false idea about yourself. You are the opposite of what you think. You are a bright, talented, committed, resilient, wonderful woman who can achieve everything you put your mind to. Nobody has told us that before. So we have to say it to each other. Watch what happens when a woman leader tells another woman she has nothing but stars on her forehead. It creates amazing growth, a current of friendship and sorority that will last forever. Put this woman in your "forever in my network" list and believe her!

Here are some key questions and self-talk phrases that can help you better manage and use your anger.

Key Questions

1. *Will being angry now help me or hurt me?* Review the discussion of positive uses of anger. Is this one of those situations? Remember that the caveman brain has its own vocabulary and its own set of goals. Once triggered, it crowds out signals from your frontal cortex, the logical, reasoning, problem-solving part of the brain. Ask yourself, will being angry now help me perform this activity or make this decision? Is there a risk that I will say or do something I will regret (including confronting someone more powerful than me)? Will being angry detract from the energy and focus I'll need for my next meeting? If you realize that being angry now will hurt you, use techniques, including self-talk phrases given here and relaxation techniques, to calm yourself.

2. *Will my anger have useful impact on this situation?* In his seminars, my colleague Sandy Smith asks participants to name all the inanimate objects they get angry at. After some laughter, responses typically include the weather, cars, lawnmowers, golf balls, golf clubs, tennis rackets, alarm clocks, TVs, appliances, tires, computers, and vending machines. Sandy then asks, "Do any of these things care that you are angry?" Often, this humorous question jolts the participants into examining just what they are accomplishing when they get angry at "things." If you are stuck in traffic and late for an appointment and let yourself get angry and upset, what happens? In addition to arriving at the meeting late, you are now upset. You've let one problem cause another problem.

3. *Am I "stewing" or doing?* This is similar to the distinction between worrying and planning. Stewing does very little good and potentially a lot of harm. To go quickly from stewing to doing, ask questions such as: What can I do to turn this situation around? Is there anything I can salvage from this situation? What can I do to prevent this from happening again? What can I learn from this situation?

Useful Self-Talk for Anger

The following phrases, if you say them to yourself in the appropriate situations, can greatly reduce anger reactions. If you practice using them regularly, over time you will develop new, more useful mental habits.

1. I can achieve my goals in this situation with firmness. I can assert myself without becoming angry or demanding.

2. No one can dictate how I will feel today. No one can push my buttons except me. I have a choice in how I am going to react to this person (or this situation).

3. The only person I can ever control is myself. I can never control another person; I can only influence them. If I expect to be able to control them, I'll wind up angry or frustrated. If I accept that I can only influence someone's free choices, I'll be calmer, learn more about the person, and be more effective.

4. This is a situation over which I have no control. My anger will have no positive impact.

5. I can calmly review and critique my performance and then make improvements without calling myself names or blaming my performance on someone else.

If a situation occurs when your being too angry has clearly had a negative impact, it is an excellent opportunity for self-reflection. Usually, there is a lot to be learned. Here are some good questions to ask yourself:

- What triggered me?
- Why does this person bother me so much?
- Did I try to communicate when I was tired or stressed?
- What was my self-talk before I got angry?

To achieve self-care within a busy work schedule and possible personal commitments, we need to make it a priority and to see it is actually the foundation of what is going to make us successful. And we need skills. Rule 12 will provide you with the skills of saying no, setting boundaries, and ensuring that you are meeting at least the minimum requirements for self-care and maintaining important personal relationships.

Lisa Feiner

Lisa is the co-founder and board chair of Sharp Again Naturally (SAN), an organization that focuses on preventing, slowing the progress of, and in some cases reversing the impact of Alzheimer's disease and dementia.

Initially, after receiving her MBA, she pursued a corporate career but eventually changed direction toward the fields of nutrition and wellness. After she studied at the Institute for Integrative Nutrition, she went on to become a certified health and wellness coach. She was on the board of a long-term care and rehabilitation facility for over 10 years and volunteered with older adults, many of whom had dementia. When she heard there were causes of memory loss that people had treated and where their memory was restored, all the pieces fell into place.

At SAN, she combined her caring, compassion, and curiosity and integrated her many areas of expertise. The immediate challenge Lisa and the organization faced was dealing with the conventional wisdom at the time about Alzheimer's and dementia. Industry power brokers and entrenched "experts" rarely mentioned any practices that could prevent brain health deterioration, and restoring brain health after the onset of the disease wasn't viewed as a possibility.

Lisa, with the knowledge she gained from coaching people to higher levels of health and wellness, and her belief in the brain's neuroplasticity, became a pioneer in the field. She followed her intuition about brain health and longevity practices and challenged the narrative about the progression of the diseases.

Now it seems like every month research from many disciplines is emerging to support Lisa's advocacy of preventative and restorative practices, including nutrition and exercise, that we can all engage in to protect our brain.

Rule 11 and Rule 12 are completely aligned with the recommendations Lisa provides to her clients and through SAN's outreach. She focuses on reducing stress, increasing joy and the number of nurturing people in your life, setting boundaries on when you are available to others, combining chores with strengthening your skills (e.g., working on improving your balance while brushing your teeth), and keeping your body strong and agile to better your short-term health and your longevity.

With Lisa, "the video matches the audio" in that she practices what she believes in, that is, nutrition, fitness, yoga, meaningful work, and close relationships with family and friends. She is a great reminder to all of us of the power of making your health and the health of others a top priority.

◆

Rule 11 Self-Assessment: Develop Healthy Selfishness

Score yourself in these nine areas, with 1 being "not at all," and 5 being "all the time."

1. Despite my varied responsibilities, I make sure to set aside time for myself.

       1   2   3   4   5

2. I am doing enough to maintain my health and most important relationships.

       1   2   3   4   5

3. Someone observing my actions on a regular basis would conclude that maintaining my health is one of my top priorities.

       1   2   3   4   5

4. After periods of hard work, I set aside enough time for rest and recovery.

       1   2   3   4   5

5. I avoid "back to back to back" activities during the day by scheduling and taking breaks.

       1   2   3   4   5

6. I practice feeling grateful on a regular basis to reduce my stress and to have a clearer perspective on setbacks or disappointments.

       1   2   3   4   5

7. I know how to reduce my stress level by shifting my focus and choosing what I say to myself (self-talk).

   (1)   (2)   (3)   (4)   (5)

8. I have learned techniques to relax my body and clear my mind.

   (1)   (2)   (3)   (4)   (5)

9. I cultivate the right level of self-acceptance so I am not overly harsh with myself when I make mistakes.

   (1)   (2)   (3)   (4)   (5)

Develop Healthy Selfishness Action Plans

Use your low scores to guide you toward an action plan.

1. ....

   ....

2. ....

   ....

3. ....

   ....

CHAPTER 15

Rule 12: Control Your Calendar and Commitments

The key message of healthy selfishness is so important I am going to repeat it.

Most often in your career you do not have to choose between your well-being and your career. In fact, focusing on self-care and using your time wisely will lead to more energy, confidence, mental clarity, resilience, and emotional control. You increase your capacity to perform at high levels and decrease your chances of career-limiting mistakes like Deborah made.

If Deborah had insisted on replacing the marginal performer, said no to the task force request, and continued her Pilates class, she would have reduced her risk of appearing overwhelmed in her new role.

So let's drill down on the attitudes and skills that allow you to practice healthy selfishness. I've found it is easier for people to remember sayings, so let's revisit one of the three phrases I shared on page 23 (Chapter 3).

"If you don't have a plan for your time, someone else will."

The person who asked Deborah to join the task force had good intentions and was not trying to sabotage her. But he had no idea about her current personal or professional commitments. Her joining his task force fit with his agenda, but it was up to Deborah to discern whether it fit her priorities and schedule.

Here are some tips for handling these kinds of requests:

1. **Don't give a quick yes**. When people ask you to volunteer for projects, they often lowball how much time it will take because they want you to say yes. It is never smart to give a quick yes because that

is the equivalent of giving someone a blank check to your time. You need more time to evaluate this commitment, so ask for it.

2. **Gather information.** You need to know realistically how much time you are signing up for (are there additional responsibilities like committee assignments?) and time to reflect on whether this fits with your other priorities and schedule. So say, "I need a realistic picture of how much time this will take, and then I will review my current responsibilities to see if I have the capacity to take this on. I will get back to you in two days."

3. **Use a soft no.** A "soft no" is a no that sets limits and boundaries around your time and sends a message that you think carefully about how you commit your time. The "soft" part is that you still convey that you are a helpful, collaborative colleague.

Here are some examples of a soft no that Deborah could have used:

> "I won't be able to join the task force at this time, but I would like to support you. If we could have lunch next week, I can share what I have learned about what makes these kinds of task forces productive. I also have time to review the findings of the task force after you have produced a report."

> "I personally can't take this on, but there is a person on my team who has a lot of passion about this initiative. She has experience on task forces, and I think this would be both a growth experience for her and a good networking opportunity. I discussed the possibility with her and she is interested."

Whether you use the soft no that I recommend or another version of no, this is a key skill to develop. Many studies have confirmed that people who have difficulty saying no have increased levels of anxiety, depression, and stress.

Setting Boundaries

We have seen how learning to say no is essential for controlling our precious time and setting ourselves up for success. Equally important is developing the practice of setting boundaries.

Here are some of the fundamental areas where we need to establish and maintain clear boundaries:

Personal versus professional time. Even before COVID-19, there were powerful societal and technological trends blurring the lines between our personal and professional lives. Evenings, weekends, and vacations used to be "our" time. Sacrificing too much of this time makes it more difficult to maintain relationships and restore ourselves.

Personal space/privacy. Everyone is different in terms of where they prefer to set boundaries in these areas. However, most of us have to deal with someone in our personal or work life who invades our space and privacy. We need to make clear what is okay and what is not okay.

Roles and responsibilities. At work we need to be alert to two types of boundary crossings in the area of roles and responsibilities: 1) someone initiates activities, or starts projects related to your responsibilities and objectives; 2) someone tries to dump their responsibilities or accountabilities on you. Both should be nipped in the bud by setting and clarifying boundaries.

Boundaries for yourself. The research is clear that the masters of the media, social media, cell phones, and computers have learned how to create "addictive" activities. This is not an alarmist, exaggerated statement. We are used to using the term "addictive" to describe drug or alcohol abuse or compulsive gambling, but there are probably more of us now dealing with "stimulation" addictions. If you find you are spending too much time on screens, you may need to set a boundary with yourself. In addition to the time factor, evaluate the energy and emotional factors. Does spending too much time watching the news or certain shows or viewing social media leave you feeling more anxious or down? If so, putting away devices, limiting time, and going on a "news" diet are all healthy self-boundaries.

Warm Boundaries

In the same way that a soft no help us say no more often while softening the impact, the language of "warm boundaries" makes it easier to establish boundaries. I first heard this term from a very wise therapist, Dan Quinn, who now practices in Ashland, Oregon. Here are some examples:

"I'm not only committed to, I'm excited about the projects we are working on. And, unless there is a real emergency I will only respond to cell calls, texts, or email between 7:00 a.m. and 7:00 p.m. weekdays."

"I'm confident that the team and I can meet the budget and deadlines of the projects we agreed to in January. And I want to be clear that these additional projects you want to add were not in the original agreement. If a priority, they may require additional resources or pushing back some other timelines."

"Everything you say yes to, you say no to something else."

Most of the time we go through our day having unnecessary conversations, attending meetings we didn't need to, going on "nice to do" (versus "need to do") trips, or getting lost surfing the web. We do not have a heightened awareness of what these activities are costing us. If you really embrace this saying, though, that will change. Going forward you will see that being at the unnecessary or unproductive meeting means you will not do some of the following more important actions:

- A workout
- Time for reflection or strategic thinking
- Relationship time with a romantic partner or your children
- Networking
- Time for rest and recovery

Repeat this phrase to yourself until it becomes a mantra that you internalize and practice: *"We train other people how to treat us."*

If you have ever trained animals or watched other people do it, you know that the key to success is reinforcement: rewarding the behavior that you want more of. Unfortunately, when we allow people to marginalize us at meetings, when we give an automatic yes to requests, when we are willing to "make do" with marginal performers, holes in the org chart, and skimpy resources, we can expect a lot more marginalization, requests, and "making do" in the future.

We are "training" other people to take advantage of us. Not everyone will, but there are enough people who notice this and treat you accordingly. So this is a key reminder, and also why I've emphasized learning and using all the rules consistently.

Toxic People

When I first became a graduate student in psychology in the mid-sixties, I was fascinated by the idea of how to help people change. There was a spectrum of approaches, all the way from Freudian analysis to behavior therapy. In my research I was amazed to find a therapeutic approach that was incredibly simple and yet yielded the best results in terms of helping people to be happier and healthier. The therapist simply helped you to make a list of two types of people in your life, toxic people and nurturing people. Toxic people were defined as people who, when you spent any amount of time with them, you usually felt bad. They had ways of undermining your confidence, making you feel bad about yourself or just more anxious, pessimistic, or angry. The therapist didn't get into the whys, just the reactions.

Nurturing people were people who made you feel good. Their concern, empathy, and belief in you came through. Even if they gave you tough feedback, you could feel they cared and they believed you could grow. The therapy involved encouraging the client to either eliminate toxic people from your life or minimize the time you spent with them. And, of course, spend more time with nurturing people.

In organizations it is not always possible to avoid all contact with toxic people, but I am encouraging you to use all the skills you have learned to minimize their presence in your life.

The same applies to toxic family members. I remember a saying I once saw on someone's wall: "Friends are welcome anytime, family members by appointment." This was probably created by someone who learned these lessons.

Reclaiming Meeting Time

We can free up hours on our calendars by attending fewer meetings or ensuring that the meetings we show up to are productive. Before agreeing to attend a meeting, ask yourself the following questions.

Do we need a meeting? Before setting up a meeting or agreeing to attend, explore alternatives. Could information be shared in other ways? Would a phone call, smaller group, or shorter meeting meet our needs?

Is this meeting well planned? Establish some standards and processes before committing your time to a meeting. Is there an agenda? What preparation do I need to participate effectively? What is the purpose of the meeting, e.g., information sharing, brainstorming, decision-making, strategic planning, conflict resolution, and so on?

Do I need to be there? Most organizations are inclined to over-invite participants to meetings. Don't reinforce this practice by blindly attending. Question whether you need to be there. Could someone on your team attend? Could you attend part of the meeting? If you were at home sick today, would they still have this meeting? If the answer is yes, that might help you feel more comfortable freeing up that time.

Will this meeting be led by a *skillful* facilitator? I emphasize "skillful" because there are quite a few skills necessary to keep a meeting on track, focusing the right amount of time on the right priorities and hitting its objectives. Here is a list of these skills:

1. Managing time
2. Keeping the discussion focused and on track
3. Ensuring wide participation (avoiding dominating behavior or under-participation)
4. Closure and accountability
5. Listening skills
6. Reading verbal and nonverbal signals
7. Firm feedback skills
8. Anticipating challenges

After reading this list, please review and evaluate the meetings you attend. If certain meetings are poorly facilitated on a regular basis, either provide some feedback and coaching, recommend meeting facilitation training, or try to get out of these meetings.

The Minimums System

Of course, organizational life is demanding and none of the rules are magically going to give you the time to pamper yourself or spend as much time as you would like with friends and family. The key is to avoid putting your health and relationships at risk. We minimize that risk by at least committing to some minimal activities that maintain what we have decided is precious to us. If we dip below that minimum, these priorities can erode. So I'm going to show you how setting minimums can keep your personal and career priorities on track.

What is a minimum? A *minimum* in this context is an activity that you commit to doing in any of the key areas (core value, commitment, current priority, long-term goal) where you perceive a gap or a risk. It is a small step in the right direction that demonstrates to you and those around you that your priorities and actions are coming into alignment. It is *not* what you wish you could do if there were more hours in the day; it represents forward motion and demonstrates your commitment. Here are some examples:

- I don't like talking to the media, but it is now a bigger part of my job and I can see I am avoiding it. My minimum is that within the next two weeks I am going to talk with a CEO in my network who is effective at interacting with the media. I am going to ask her for some tips or find out about the training she received.

- Maintaining my health is one of my top priorities, but I've essentially stopped exercising. My minimum is to walk at least 30 minutes, four days a week. I'm going to accomplish this by walking to and from the train. I'm also going to use the stairs (two flights) instead of the elevator.

- I really care about environmental issues, but I haven't made any changes in my lifestyle. My minimum is to use the carpool option in my community twice a week and sign up for a newsletter on environmental action steps.

- It's important to me to maintain the romantic part of the relationship with my partner. My minimum is to keep at least one night a week for ourselves when we are not exhausted and not just trading to-do lists, when we can have fun, connect physically, or talk about what's important to us.

- I want to maintain the bonds with my children, especially as they become teenagers. Right now, between my unpredictable schedule, my travel, and their activities, we are like ships passing in the night. My minimum is to talk with each of my children 10 minutes a day, be home for a family dinner at least one night a week, and spend one hour alone with each child on the weekends.

The key to minimums is that they must be reasonable to you based on your schedule. You are going to set them (sometimes in discussion with the other people involved) and commit to them.

Another powerful way to look at minimums is to consider the consequences of not meeting those you have designated. By setting a minimum, you are saying this is a very important area of your life. You are saying this is the minimum you need to do to support it; you are saying this is a small-enough commitment that you can definitely do it. So, if you don't achieve your minimum, what does it mean? You might have to admit:

- It is not really a priority.
- You are willing to conduct your life in a way that puts this area at risk.
- You are overcommitted and need to make some changes.

By now you should be able to see both the more obvious and the more subtle benefits of setting and scheduling minimums.

- *Progress, not perfection:* A very high percentage of people follow through on their minimums when they focus on a small-enough step, which they have designated and committed to, and for which they have allotted a place in their schedule. This leads to further steps in a positive direction and an increase in self-esteem. It also means they are keeping promises and are predictable in a positive way.

- *A warning system:* A minimum is an obvious marker. If you start missing your minimums, it will quickly be apparent to you and the people around you. This will help you get back on track rapidly. Without this warning system, you are vulnerable to the law of gradual change, and your alignment gap may grow wider. The minimums system is your "canary in the coal mine," signaling to you that you are neglecting an important area in your life.

- *Self-knowledge and self-awareness:* Consistently missing your minimums is not a good sign, but it usually leads to deeper reflection on the root causes of failure, which is a good thing. Ask yourself:
  - Did I neglect to schedule my minimums on my calendar?
  - Was I overly optimistic about what I committed to?
  - Am I diverting time to lower-priority activities?
  - Am I overcommitted and do I need to revisit some of my current obligations?
  - Are my demanding job and my inability to set limits and boundaries combining to thwart my best intentions?

The point in creating minimums in key areas is that you gain no matter what the outcome. Either you set yourself on a positive trajectory or you identify the significant behaviors you need to change, the skills you need to acquire, or the decisions you need to make.

Combining versus Multitasking

When we multitask we are trying (usually not that well) to do more than one thing at the same time. Combining is a much more useful skill because it allows us to accomplish multiple goals with one activity. Here are some examples of combining:

- Conducting a business discussion while walking
- Watching a useful video or reading while riding a stationary bike
- Walking while reflecting or doing strategic thinking
- Exercising with a friend, family member, or someone in your network
- Social interest work (Habitat for Humanity, beach cleanup) with your children, which combines values, light exercise, and time together

Use your creativity to come up with ways to spend quality time with friends, family, and romantic partners while advancing other goals around fitness, rest, recovery, fresh air, nature, and so on. My personal example is teaching my daughter to play tennis. This achieved quite a few important things:

- It was a fitness activity for both of us.
- She became proficient in an activity that built her confidence and joined a team in high school that provided friends and leadership opportunities.
- She learned about practice, errors, and calm self-critique.
- We had good conversations driving to and from playing tennis, and it helped me keep up with what was going on in her life.

◆

Rule 12 Self-Assessment: Control Your Calendar and Commitments

Score yourself in these five areas, with 1 being "not at all," and 5 being "all the time."

1. Before I say yes to requests for my time, I carefully evaluate the time required and how this decision would impact my current commitments.

    (1)   (2)   (3)   (4)   (5)

2. I can politely and skillfully say no to requests for my time.

    (1)   (2)   (3)   (4)   (5)

3. I have systems to alert me when I am getting out of alignment with my values and personal priorities.

    (1)   (2)   (3)   (4)   (5)

4. I understand that "everything I say yes to, I am saying no to something else," so I carefully evaluate requests for my time.

    (1)   (2)   (3)   (4)   (5)

5. For me, meeting effectiveness is a work-life balance issue, because time wasted at unproductive meetings may cause me to work longer hours.

    (1)   (2)   (3)   (4)   (5)

Control Your Calendar and Commitments Action Plans

Use your low scores to guide you toward an action plan.

1. ....

    ....

2. ....

    ....

3. ....

    ....

Key 12 Rules Sayings

- Is a great leader loved or feared?
- If you have power, you may not be as smart, funny, or attractive as people are telling you.
- You don't have to floss all your teeth, just the ones you want to keep.
- "When someone shows you who they are, believe them the first time." —Maya Angelou
- "My life has been a series of horrible misfortunes, most of which never happened." —Mark Twain
- "We convince by our presence." —Walt Whitman
- "Care about what others think and you will always be their prisoner." —Lao-tzu
- The day you need a network it's too late to build it.
- The difference between reality and perception is that people make decisions based on perception.
- People will tell you how to sell them.
- If you don't have a plan for your time, someone else will.
- We train other people how to treat us.
- Everything you say yes to, you say no to something else.
- Does the video match the audio?
- The most important sale you will ever make is to sell yourself first.
- You can't lose what you don't have.
- You already paid for the lesson so you might as well get the learning.

CHAPTER 16

The 12 Rules for Women of Color

The 12 Rules is uniquely suited to ensure success for women of color (WOC). Through the years I have had the pleasure of meeting and interacting with hundreds of leaders and aspiring leaders across a vast array of global industries. My long career as a global HR executive has provided me an opportunity to speak with thousands of women, and I have found that many were dangerously naive about the world of work. It was commonplace to hear that many were schooled as youth to put faith in doing the right thing, seeing the good in others, working the hardest, and relying on the belief that results will carry the day or speak for themselves. Sadly, many learned, painfully, as adults, that was just not the case and, more often than not, realized that success was due to factors having nothing to do with meritocracy.

Women of color face the challenges of gender along with their female colleagues but also are confronted with added difficulties of race, ethnicity, and cultural biases. Over 50 years ago, Frances Beal referred to this condition as "double jeopardy." The intersection of gender and race, ethnicity, and culture is often confusing and perplexing. What's more, women of color often exist in very different, often competing worlds, both professionally and personally.

Women of color must learn to navigate power dynamics and challenges of gender, race, ethnicity, and culture, often simultaneously. They routinely face biases (some conscious, some unconscious) uniquely targeting their differences from their white male colleagues and from leadership. It is common to face gender/race/ethnicity/culturally based accusations that are not levied at white men: "angry black women," "hypersensitivity," "overly emotional, hot-tempered Latina women," "quiet, polite Asian women," and so on.

Trying to differentiate between motivations of gender or race inequalities is not easy. Women of color regularly experience both simultaneously and often struggle with which one is the predominant challenge to overcome. An added hurdle is when the intersection of gender and race places WOC at risk of undesirable behaviors from members of their same gender as well as same race, ethnicity, or culture.

Suffering the burdens of gender can be demoralizing and, when combined with race, ethnicity, and culture, even more so. How many long-standing, seemingly successful relationships among women were shattered when issues of race were raised? I recall a discussion of the January 6, 2021, attack on Congress between two female executives, one white and one black, who cherished their long-standing friendship. The white female executive boldly compared the actions of the insurgents to those of the Black Lives Matter protesters. She confidently stated that both groups had violated the law and should be treated as criminals. Shocked by the comparison, the black female executive explained the difference by stating that the Black Lives Matter protesters were exercising their lawfully protected right to engage in peaceful protest without the use of violence. The white female executive continued to assert that there was no difference between the actions of the groups. Shocked and personally offended by the attitude of her "friend," the black female executive ended the discussion by stating that her white female "friend" clearly didn't understand the issues and expressed disappointment that her white friend didn't really know her as a black woman at all. The long-standing relationship abruptly ended.

Where do women of color and the intersection of race and gender fit? Do they have the experiences, expectations, and aspirations more similar to their white female counterparts or are they more akin to men of color? One thing is for sure: Women of color and white women travel different paths as they attempt to navigate the challenges of corporate America.

In chapter 2, you learned that there are four disadvantages that often hobble the pace and progression of women's careers. The skills and concepts of the 12 Rules are needed to remove those vulnerabilities.

If that is the case for all women, let's look at the importance of the 12 Rules through the lens of these findings:

1. Women make 79 cents on the dollar compared to men for comparable work. For African American women it's 64 cents, for Latinas 54 cents.

2. WOC constitute 18 percent of the US population but hold only 4 percent of C-suite roles.

3. In the US, in 50 percent of households with children under 18, the breadwinner is a woman. For African American women, it's 80 percent.

4. A 2006 survey of employees at five large US companies found that WOC were the group most likely to experience workplace harassment.

5. A McKinsey/LeanIn.org study revealed that WOC were less likely to have bosses who promoted their work contributions, assigned them visible projects, or purposefully included them in key networks.

It is for these reasons that it is critically important that women of color embrace the groundbreaking 12 Rules practices to improve their chances of survival and success in their professional and personal lives. Learning to master the 12 Rules will undoubtedly have a game-changing effect.

In this chapter we will explore how studying power, leveraging an effective network of allies and advocates, and understanding how image and "buzz" contribute to success. We will also learn why it is important to hone skills of detection for purposes of protection, the value of recognizing the real success scorecard, and other skills that are critically important to ensure career and personal success.

Rule 1: Study Power

For women of color, studying power is a skill and life lesson that is often taught, and it must be learned from an early age. Parents of color teach their children tactics to survive in a world known to be unkind to people most unlike those in power. So, it's critical to understand the power dynamics and know who is in power. This skill is easily transferred to the work environment. Interestingly enough, women of color do not leverage their existing skills in this area, oftentimes fearing that it would appear to be manipulative.

Power is manifested in a number of ways: through language (verbal and nonverbal), physical positioning in a meeting, public acknowledgment (either positive or negative), and deference or dismissive behavior. I am often fascinated by the degree to which women listen very carefully to what is being said but fail to observe the behaviors of the speaker or members of the listening audience or those they are seeking to influence. Much is to be gleaned by doing so.

Is power singularly focused or shared more broadly? Knowing the critical difference is of utmost importance because not knowing could put you at risk of falling victim to the tactics of those seeking to manipulate you or the circumstances surrounding you.

The ability to "read the room" is highly regarded and is a critical skill highly sought after in leaders. Such skills are rewarded in not-so-subtle ways (access to or membership in closed networks of powerful people, plumb assignments, high pay, and so on). A common mistake is to recognize only positional power and not seek to understand how power is used (or misused), and influence leveraged within their environment.

I remember watching a heated debate among MBA students at a top Ivy League graduate management program. When asked to name the most powerful employees in an organization, students mentioned the CEO, president, CFO, and a variety of other C-suite positions. One lone individual offered secretaries. Laughter ensued until the professor asked for an explanation. The student, who had extensive work experience, began to explain that the job of secretaries is to act as a gatekeeper, thus granting access— or not—to powerful leaders and having access to critically important information long before it becomes public. Many a career has been made or devastated by these often-underestimated individuals.

The ability to gauge individuals with influence and impact is a critical skill for leaders and aspiring leaders. Studying "power" enables women to understand the organizational dynamics of influence to advance positive initiatives and outcomes both organizationally and individually, while minimizing the possibility of marginalization and stolen credit for successful ideas, and protecting oneself and the organization from more devious intentions.

Equally important is understanding the difference between, and being able to recognize, Power Over and Power With behaviors. The first can manifest itself in undesirable ways including controlling, demanding, and abusive behaviors that discourage collaboration, transparency, and the open exchanges of ideas. Leaders demonstrating these characteristics are often viewed negatively, or at least suspiciously, by staff and coworkers. Creativity is stymied and "speaking truth to power" discouraged or, worse yet, punished. Power Over leaders are those who carefully manage the airwaves and who focus more on creating or sustaining a self-serving narrative than leveraging the talents of their staff. On the other hand, leaders who leverage a Power With approach have a more collaborative expectation of themselves and others, and have an uncanny ability to create an environment of innovative, creative thought leaders who courageously challenge the status quo and embrace a culture of continuous learning.

Equally as important in studying power is learning what matters most to the powerful. Understanding their values and priorities—or success "scorecard"—is critical to knowing how best to spend time and invest personal energy and organizational resources. A misstep in this area could be costly both personally and organizationally. It is always fascinating to hear aspiring leaders describe the strategic priorities of their organization and those of their leaders as one in the same. Sometimes this is true, but more often it is not. Knowing and understanding the difference can make or break careers. I have coached a number of women who still feel that "working hard" and achieving published strategic priorities are all that matter, only to find themselves being passed over and standing outside the coveted "inner circle." When asked to describe their understanding of the leadership scorecard, they routinely refer to the laminated wallet card of the organization's published values and principles. When then asked to comment on who has been promoted over a six- to twelve-month period, they describe people whose behaviors are completely opposite the values and principles listed on the laminated card. Often it is only then that the individuals realize there is a big difference between published organizational priorities and the *actual* leadership scorecard. How many times have organizations demonstrated that while they promote diversity, equity, and inclusion, they continue to appoint the same profile of individuals to coveted positions of leadership? While extolling a commitment to customer-centered initiatives, individuals more focused on internal, operational, or financially focused priorities are celebrated and rewarded. Studying the pattern of those recognized and rewarded is key to understanding what matters most to senior leaders, the "real scorecard."

In 2019 a top HR executive for an academic medical center, while speaking with a very results-oriented black woman in healthcare, explained how, despite her repeated success in achieving the goals of her department leader, she never quite received the same level of recognition and rewards as her less successful coworker. When asked why she thought that had occurred, she attempted to explain in painstaking detail that it was due to obvious bias on the part of her leader. When pressed to describe the attributes of the leader and, more importantly, what the leader valued most, the clinician shared that the leader took pride in being a visionary, big-picture thinker, placing little or no value on tactical details. The clinician then expressed frustration that her coworker also spent little time on the details of an initiative, preferring to talk only about broader, big-picture concepts. It was then that the light came on. The clinician stopped while comparing the two and expressed shock at the similarities.

Lastly, it is to be understood that power is fluid and may change or shift over time. It is critically important to recognize this point and adjust accordingly. Too many times members of a once-revered power group have found themselves on the outside fighting for their survival when the powerful leader is dethroned. Women and those of color are particularly vulnerable should this happen. Often they are the last to know when a shift is occurring because they lack access to critical information needed to fully understand and anticipate the organizational and individual impact.

In summary, women (particularly those of color) cannot afford to shy away from becoming astute at studying power. Doing so means one must gain deep understanding of who is among the powerful, what their behavioral dynamics are, what matters most on their scorecard of success, and lastly, prepare oneself for a possible shift so as not to get caught in the cross fire.

Now that you have an appreciation for the need to study power, what do you do with the information once you have it?

Rule 2: Detect to Protect

How does one discern a difference between power that advantages the greater good and power that detracts from it? Women, who are often encouraged to see the best in people, can be vulnerable to dishonorable people who demonstrate a pattern of self-serving actions and behaviors.

Throughout my more than 30-year career as an HR executive, I have been fascinated by the fact that more often than not men tend to see people for who they are, and women see people for who they believe they can be. Such an approach may cause one to trust too soon, rationalize, and quickly forgive bad behavior as one-offs. This generosity is offered even in the face of a predictable pattern of undesirable or bad behavior. I am always amazed at how women resist the notion that some individuals are dishonorable and care only about advancing their agendas, even at the expense of others or the organization.

How does one detect and protect oneself from such individuals? It starts with understanding how to assess patterns of behaviors to determine trustworthiness. Assessing behaviors (most of which are highly predictable) is a skill when, well honed, is highly valued.

Who knew that a childhood favorite, "Little Red Riding Hood," was more than a fairy tale but rather foreshadowed what would become a career challenge? I have lost count of the number of people I've encountered throughout my career who were really wolves in sheep's clothing, representing themselves as supporters, mentors, and champions, only to find their intentions to be at best self-serving and at worst destructive. Their charade of support and mentoring is nothing more than a form of manipulation and control to advance their agenda. What is particularly disturbing is that these people often benefit from being entrusted with highly sensitive and potentially damaging facts and insights from their unknowing victims. Victims are lulled into a false sense of safety and transparency after falling for the wolves' sheeplike exterior. While victims may begin to suspect the different behaviors, they resist acknowledging the existence of a more sinister motive.

Women and people of color are particularly vulnerable to this scheme. At times, under the guise of diversity, equity, and inclusion champions, some individuals use this designation to advance themselves and their agendas for greater access to powerful and influential leaders.

These individuals exhibit predictable behaviors, share attributes as master manipulators, and have a high need for control of decision making, messaging, resources, and access to power. They also share a fear of exposure. They seek to discredit those who hold vital but potentially damaging information about their true agendas by intimidating or silencing truth tellers, limiting access to powerful leaders, or tormenting the truth tellers to run them out of the organization.

At a conference of black female high-potential middle managers, a participant told the story of a well-known, highly regarded global operations leader who routinely discouraged team members from speaking with finance or HR professionals within the organization. The conference participant went on to share that upon the retirement of the global operations leader, it was discovered that he was using departmental finance resources to fund the construction of various homes, hobbies, family vacations, and more. When department members were asked if they knew about these practices, the response was that it was a widely known fact, but no one dared to expose the truth for fear of the leader's wrath, influence with powerful executives, and retaliatory reach.

This example makes clear that the global operations leader, while publicly held in high regard, was well known for his focus on self-serving agendas, putting his self-interest above the interests of the organization, employees, and shareholders.

When the conference participant was asked what could have been done to protect herself, others, and the organization from the global operations leader's actions and the predictable outcome, her response was equally as predictable. She sought reasons to excuse his behavior rather than hold him accountable for his actions. She spoke eloquently in her attempt to rationalize his behavior as being somehow justified by matters outside his control.

An important lesson learned from this and countless other similar experiences is to leverage the advice of Dr. Maya Angelou, who said, "When someone shows you who they are, believe them the first time." How does one do so and how does one protect themselves and the best interests of their organization? Memorizing and using the behavior charts in Rule 2 is a great place to start.

Rule 4: Know Your Buzz

While I was conducting a coaching session in 2018 with a small group of female nurse leaders, one participant shared her point of view about talent-related discussions held without the presence of the employee being discussed. She characterized the situation by stating, "If you're not at the table, you may be on the menu." No truer words were ever spoken.

Talent review discussions are held both formally and informally in a variety of formats across all industries and organizations. Sadly, many of these discussions are often based on soundbites and anecdotes, rather than facts, tangible results, and outcomes. Women, and those of color may find themselves the subject of these discussions without prior knowledge and only learn about it after the fact. If they are lucky, someone will share the perceptions disclosed of their talent assessment, performance, perceived leadership attributes, and growth potential. More often than not, though, they will remain unaware of how they are perceived by the organization.

The image one projects—either knowingly or unknowingly, intentionally or not—can have a direct effect on your buzz and/or your reputation. WOC must be particularly attentive and conscious of how they are perceived because of the influence that unfounded or unsubstantiated gender, race, and/or ethnicity stereotypes and biases may play. Particular vulnerabilities include age-old stereotypical accusations about aggressiveness, overconfidence, hypersensitivity, and the inability to control one's emotions, to name a few. Without knowing it, one could find oneself validating negative perceptions on the one hand and discrediting positive buzz on the other.

It is for this reason that it is critically important for women of color to care how they are perceived and what is discussed or disclosed about them in conversations both positive and negative. I often ask individuals and group participants how many people know how they are perceived and what is said about them when they are not present. Not surprisingly, many are unaware of their buzz. Others stated that they were aware of falsehoods about them but attributed them to misunderstandings or personality conflicts with coworkers or supervisors. If you are lucky enough to be the subject of positive buzz, it is more important to emphasize the strengths while developing a plan to minimize accentuating negative perceptions. Women of color should not underestimate the power of leveraging buzz to advance their agenda, initiatives, and their careers.

From my HR perspective, everyone in corporations could benefit from more accurate, timely, and useful feedback. Most of us don't receive enough because our managers haven't been trained to do it effectively and are not comfortable delivering it. For WOC, this is compounded by managers concerned about being perceived as biased. As a result, we often don't get the guidance and timely course corrections we need.

Gaining insight into how one is perceived is not easy. The information can come in a variety of forms and through a variety of forums. The most obvious is through a formal performance appraisal discussion. But beware, because many supervisors find giving feedback to be uncomfortable, particularly for women of color. WOC may find themselves needing to solicit feedback by explaining their interest in and personal commitment to continuous improvement.

Pay attention to seemingly throwaway comments that speak to consistent behavioral examples. They can be a source of insights about image or buzz. For example, "Sally is very tactical" might mean "Sally lacks strategic vision," or "Mary is tough and tenacious" might mean "Mary lacks sensitivity or the ability to build consensus." Other insights are often shared through humorous comments, but they are not to be taken lightly.

Once you know your buzz, what should you do about it? If it is positive, lean into it. Continue to accentuate what works and what is highly regarded by leadership, customers, staff, and others. If it is negative, be cognizant and develop a plan to counter behaviors or stereotypes feeding the misconceptions.

Leverage allies, advocates, and members of your network to help promote your buzz and counter negative perceptions. This is when having done the prework of establishing an effective network will pay the greatest dividends. It is at this time when you will most need a network—and then it's too late to build one.

Rule 5: Focus on the Real Scorecard

It's commonly understood that actions speak louder than words. The same holds true in the work environment. Strangely enough, though, I have witnessed women resist applying this principle.

While much is written in leadership bulletins and announcements, far more is disclosed when women pay attention to who gets promoted, publicly recognized (or shamed), and rewarded. A careful review is needed of their behaviors, results, and the programs and initiatives they support (or don't support). This is an important step toward understanding the real scorecard, the expectations of leadership, and, most importantly, what are considered to be the desirable traits and core competencies.

Rule 6: Leverage Your Network

One of the most important and powerful tools in the success arsenal for women of color is an effective network of advocates and allies. These individuals are committed to and supportive of WOC's success, operating in their best interest and providing valuable insights about the organization, current and future leaders, key initiatives, and strategic priorities.

Despite the advances of gender empowerment and women leaders, the work environment continues to be very much a boys' club. Women of color, in particular, often find themselves fewer in number than their white counterparts and in need of allies and advocates. As a result, it is imperative that they establish an effective network of individuals with influence and impact who possess a wide range of diversity, including gender, race, and ethnicity. Their network should contain individuals from all levels of the organization and those with access to key leaders, decision-makers, and critical information.

Ensuring a high-quality network of advocates and allies is a deliberate and strategic activity. The goal is to establish key contacts who have access to individuals with the power to allocate resources and approval to advance your career agenda and initiatives. Women often express discomfort with the need to deliberately orchestrate relationships of influence. It may feel manipulative and inauthentic. On the contrary, there are benefits to be gained from having the right circle of influence. In short, what you don't know can kill your career.

When it comes to building a network, some people are clearly more valuable than others. Here's what I look for:

- Can I trust that this person has good intentions?
- Does their information tend to be accurate?
- Are they "wired in"?
- Does this person get to hear the "hidden dialogue"?

The "hidden dialogue" refers to what men may say about women when they are not present or what white people may say about people of color in similar circumstances.

I also need people in my network purely for support: people who can validate me, remind me of my strengths, and allow me to vent (as long as I don't do it too often).

Rule 8: Self-Promotion

Considering that, as noted earlier, your bosses are less likely to promote your accomplishments, please practice the techniques you read about in chapter 10. In particular I think WOC need to focus on and remind ourselves of all our strengths.

- Think about the wisdom you have accumulated over your life.
- Look at the challenges you have met and overcome.
- Credit yourself for what you have done with the opportunities you had.

Of course I don't know your life circumstances, but many of us have had to maximize the chances we encountered to be in the position we are in today. Such was not the case for the privileged few. As Kerry Washington says to Reese Witherspoon in *Little Fires Everywhere*, "You didn't make good choices, you had good choices."

Rule 9: Executive Presence

We know we need to have a seat at the table, that people need to hear our voice. Certainly we need to be confident and, at times, forceful leaders. In addition, we sometimes hear the advice to be "authentic" and "speak your truth."

How do we balance these goals against the concern of being labeled as angry or having a chip on your shoulder?

Thirty years ago my manager sent me to Marty for executive coaching. Marty is someone who hears the "hidden dialogue," and in our first meeting he told me that my boss described me as "an angry young woman." Marty and I have been friends for a long time. Over the years he has shared with me that he has coached hundreds of forceful, aggressive people, but he has only heard African American women described as "angry." Each of you needs to find this balance, this "narrow path," for yourself. For me, the advice in chapter 11 is useful and effective.

I strive to stay calm and centered. My self-talk reminds me that "no one can dictate how I'm going to feel today. No one can push my buttons but me." I use the right vocabulary to be firm, clear, and say what is acceptable. Very often I document what is communicated because I may need it at a later time.

Rule 10: Protecting Yourself from Sabotage and Marginalization

In addition to the protective phrases you learned in chapter 12, I would like you to be extra prepared for a certain combination of marginalization, microaggression, and gaslighting that often comes our way. I want to be sure you see this coming.

Here is the scenario: At a meeting someone will tease, provoke, or disrespect you (marginalization/microaggression). Then, when you respond, here come the gaslighting phrases:

- "Why are you getting upset?"
- "Calm down."
- "I'm just kidding. Why are you so sensitive?"
- "You take everything so personally."
- "You have a chip on your shoulder."

My strategy: Stay calm, centered, clear, firm.

Rules 11 & 12: Self-Care and Healthy Selfishness

Self-care is a political act. —Audre Lorde

With the challenges we routinely face in balancing our professional and personal lives—including caring for family (immediate and extended), the household, childcare, and eldercare—these two rules become a path to survival. Many of us have developed patterns of putting our needs last. I don't need to repeat all these valuable and, in some cases, life-changing tips in Rules 11 and 12. I'm just emphasizing them and asking you to make them a priority. Even though they are the last two rules, I feel that for many of you reading this book they should be the first two!

CHAPTER 17

Men, Our Key Allies

The last century has seen human progress, advances, and victories, but not one country has achieved gender equality. Women have struggled to achieve workforce equality, and more and more men have joined the effort. When women work, there are undeniable returns—to their families, communities, and national economies. Yet gender inequality is everywhere.

Men are not always part of this discussion, but they're a critical part of the solution. Because men are in many more positions of power within the workplace, they have the opportunity and responsibility to help shift culture by applying policies that will help balance the agenda. Relegating equality to a "women's issue" perpetuates the notion that only women will benefit from a more equal society. It's essential that men are aware of how gender equality will benefit everyone and that they know gender equality can only be achieved when both men and women shift norms.

Fortunately, the world is full of amazing men who are sponsors, mentors, and strong advocates of this agenda. It is clear to us that to make progress we need men fully involved. Both women and men are part of the solution.

We need more men to challenge and change gender bias in policies, practices, and cultural norms. Furthermore, women need men to mentor and sponsor their career paths to gain more access to the highest levels of leadership. While 48 percent of men report that they've received detailed career path advice in the last two years, only 15 percent of women say the same. Further, while 54 percent of men had a career discussion with a mentor or sponsor, only 39 percent of women report the same.[36]

Gender equality isn't a women's issue; it's a business issue. Companies can benefit from investing in women as leaders, employees, entrepreneurs, customers, and community partners. Expanding and strengthening women's workforce participation and leadership results in improved human capital, enhanced market demand, and an equal opportunity environment.

Imagine a world where gender equality is the norm. Classrooms, boardrooms, courtrooms, and political offices are filled equally with men and women. Men are able and even encouraged to take paid leave to be with their newborn infant or a sick child. Women and men are paid the same for the same work. Imagine a world where this kind of equality shapes decisions that affect our lives, bodies, health, and environment. This is a world where people have equal rights and opportunities. To achieve this reality, women and men need to discuss and troubleshoot diversity, equality, and inclusion issues in the workplace.

Studies show that female leaders spend more time than their male counterparts on diversity, equity, and inclusion (DEI). Women at the senior level are twice as likely to spend time focused on DEI at least twice a week. This is work that often falls outside of the realm of their usual job responsibilities, and can include tasks like supporting employee resource groups or actively recruiting staff from underrepresented groups.[37] Male leaders can—and should—join, too, yet they are underrepresented at the equality table. They can listen and ask for recommendations in order to co-shape corporate policies on DEI. If there aren't DEI networks, men who have leadership positions can help create space and opportunity for them to develop.

One significant issue is that women provide a disproportionate amount of all childcare. In 2018, 606 million women of working age were unavailable for employment owing to childcare responsibilities, compared to just 41 million men.[38] Changes in policy are needed to decrease the double shift that often burdens women. Men can be part of the change by helping promote paid paternity leave that is of equal length to that afforded women. They can help shift the culture to promote more flexible work hours. They can also lead the way in taking advantage of these policies and promoting them among the men in their offices, so that when a man becomes a father, he doesn't question whether he should take paternity leave, but instead plans on it.

Men as Sponsors

Gender equality is fundamentally a question of power. Understanding power is a task for both sexes, and it's critical that we all recognize the web of relationships that affects power and how that shapes performance, decisions, and outcomes. Organizations and leaders have looked for years at why women aren't making it to the top for years. The reality has to do with power—what it can do for you when you have the right connections . . . or not.

Sponsorship is not to be confused with mentoring. Mentors can be sponsors, but sponsors are much more than mentors. Sponsorship specifically focuses on advancements and links to power. A sponsor is someone who has considerable decision-making power, influence on processes and structures, and who is advocating for, protecting, and fighting for the career advancement of an individual.[39] Sponsors leverage their own reputational capital and positional power to recommend high-performing employees for opportunities and promotions.

This kind of visibility is needed for female candidates because, as mentioned earlier, women are often just overlooked. Recently, the Center for Talent Innovation reported that 71 percent of executives have protégés whose gender and race match their own.[40] Furthermore, studies show that women who advocate for themselves can be penalized.[41] Sponsorship helps women avoid this double bind.

This type of leveraging is critically important for women. When women's mentors are highly placed, that is, a sponsor, they're just as likely as men to be promoted.[42] Unlike a mentor, a sponsor does much more than give career advice or feedback. A sponsor can propel a candidate, accelerate their career, and open up access to networks. Like a mentor, sponsors give advice, but the difference is that the advice is usually targeted, actionable, and meant to help the person stretch into a role or assignment that the sponsor recommended for them. This is especially true at the executive level and when the sponsor understands the long-term career goals of their protégé.

While sponsorship can open doors, it's still the protégé's responsibility to deliver. Opportunities don't guarantee success. Trust is needed for the sponsor to promote you because they need to know you will do a good job. Protégés also need to trust that a sponsor has their best interests in mind. The most successful sponsorships use, create, and build reputational capital for both the sponsor and the protégé. We encourage male leaders to keep this in mind and to look for that spark that makes them think a person can do more—and then help them do that.

Women need sponsorship to tip the scales and continue climbing that leadership ladder. While many women at the top are taking on this role, men are needed too. There are simply not enough women in the leadership ranks to transfer power to the next generation of women.

Men as Mentors

Sponsorship and mentoring are both critical for improving gender imbalances in the workplace, especially on leadership teams. Mentors may not have the same reputational capital, decision-making influence, or power, but they often have more power than they use. They provide guidance for career choices and decisions, and even help a mentee figure out a path to meet a career goal. Mentors often support their mentees in private but don't always actively advocate for them.

Still, mentors are critical. When women are mentored, they're better prepared for promotions and have higher success rates. They tend to stay with their organizations for longer periods of time because they're more satisfied with their careers. Perhaps most importantly, women rate higher on performance measures when they're mentored because they're perceived as more innovative and creative. Mentorship helps mentees be more resilient and develop stronger networks.

While mentoring is critical at all stages of career development, sponsors are necessary for taking the next step to advocating on behalf of women for advancement into leadership roles.

Men Opening Doors for Women

Fortune 500 companies with the highest representation of women on their boards outperform those with the fewest women.[43] Yet, in many companies, too few women reach the top. As a result, women and companies are missing out. If companies want to increase diversity and improve their financial results, talent needs to be developed at all levels of the organization. Mentoring and sponsorship are good for business and for women.

Developing mentors and sponsors to help women navigate their careers will help stop the leaky pipeline of female talent. If women are going to join the leadership ranks and have the same access to career and growth opportunities as men, they need the help of both mentors and sponsors. The only way to achieve gender parity in leadership is with women having equal power and opportunity.

The authors of this book—and many of the women we profiled—have had the privilege of having great male sponsors and mentors. We are surrounded, starting with Marty, by men who are passionate about this agenda and also see the solid benefits that female talent has for businesses, and communities overall.

Let's spread the word and make sure that many more leaders, men and women, join and accelerate this journey of women's empowerment.

Notes

1. World Bank, *Jobs for Shared Prosperity: Time for Action in the Middle East and North Africa*, 2013, https://openknowledge.worldbank.org/handle/10986/13284.
2. Jonathan Woetzel, et al., McKinsey Global Institute, *How Advancing Women's Equality Can Add $12 Trillion to Global Growth*, 2015.
3. International Monetary Fund, *Pursuing Women's Economic Empowerment*, 2018, https://www.imf.org/en/Publications/Policy-Papers/Issues/2018/05/31/pp053118pursuing-womens-economicempowerment.
4. McKinsey & Company, *Women Matter: Time to Accelerate. Ten Years of Insights into Gender Diversity*, 2018, https://www.empowerwomen.org/-/media/files/un percent20women/empowerwomen/resources/hlp percent20briefs/unhlp percent20full percent20report.pdf?la=en.
5. OECD Statistics are from the Online Employment Database. https://stats.oecd.org/Index.aspx?DataSetCode=lfs_sexage_i_r
6. Sun, Sophia. (29 April 2021). *Covid-19 costs women $800 billion in lost income.* news.trust.org. Retrieved October 4, 2021, from https://news.trust.org/item/20210429073049-8e92a.
7. Heintz, J., Turquet, L., & Staab, S. (2021, March 1). *Don't let another crisis go to waste: The COVID-19 pandemic and the imperative for a paradigm shift.* Taylor & Francis. Retrieved October 4, 2021, from https://www.tandfonline.com/doi/full/10.1080/13545701.2020.1867762.
8. With the term working women, we assume the definition of a woman working for salary or wages outside of the home. We recognize this while simultaneously acknowledging that women have also and still carry the double burden of care and work at home.
9. Jacobs, E., & Bahn, K. (March 22, 2019). *Women's History Month: U.S. Women's Labor Force Participation. Equitable Growth.* Retrieved October 4, 2021, from https://equitablegrowth.org/womens-history-month-u-s-womens-labor-force-participation/.
10. Yellen, J. L. (2021, January 6). *The history of women's work and wages and how it has created success for us all.* Brookings. Retrieved October 4, 2021, from https://www.brookings.edu/essay/the-history-of-womens-work-and-wages-and-how-it-has-created-success-for-us-all/.
11. Jacobs & Bahn, 2019.
12. University of Pennsylvania, "To Close the Gender Gap, What Needs to Change — Women or the System?", May 27, 2013, available at http://knowledge.wharton.upenn.edu/article.cfm?articleid=3219.
13. Susan Ehrlich Martin and Nancy Jurik, "Women Entering the Legal Profession: Change and Resistance." In Susan Ehrlich Martin and Nancy Jurik, eds., Doing Justice, Doing Gender (Thousand Oaks, CA: Sage Publications, 2007), available at http://www.sagepub.com/upm-data/12634_Chapter5.pdf.
14. Feminist Majority Foundation, "Empowering Women in Medicine," available at http://www.feminist.org/research/medicine/ewm_toc.html.

15. Committee for Economic Development, "Fulfilling the Promise: How More Women on Corporate Boards Would Make America and American Companies More Competitive" (2012), available at http://www.fwa.org/pdf/CED_WomenAdvancementonCorporateBoards.pdf.

16. Yellen, 2021.

17. National Center for Education Statistics, "Table 318.30. Bachelor's, master's, and doctor's degrees conferred by postsecondary institutions, by sex of student and discipline," available at https://nces.ed.gov/programs/digest/d16/tables/dt16_318.30.asp.

18. The Association to Advance Collegiate Schools of Business, "2016 Business School Data Guide" (2016), available at http://www.aacsb.edu/-/media/aacsb/publications/data-trends-booklet/2016.ashx.

19. Sun, 2021.

20. McKinsey & Company, 2021.

21. United Nations Human Rights Office. (2021, July 27). *We must prioritize a gender-responsive recovery from COVID-19.* Retrieved October 4, 2021, from https://www.ohchr.org/EN/NewsEvents/Pages/Women-Covid19.aspx.

22. *Women as drivers of economic recovery and resilience during COVID-19 and beyond.* UN Women. (2020, July 14). Retrieved October 4, 2021, from https://www.unwomen.org/en/news/stories/2020/7/statement-joint-w20-women-during-covid-19-and-beyond.

23. Ibid.

24. Sun, 2021.

25. Coffey, C., Espinoza Revollo, P., Harvey, R., Lawson, M., Parvez Butt, A., Piaget, K., Sarosi, D., & Thekkudan, J. (2020). (rep.). *Time to Care: Unpaid and underpaid care work and the global inequality crisis.* Oxfam. Retrieved October 4, 2021, from https://oxfamilibrary.openrepository.com/bitstream/handle/10546/620928/bp-time-to-care-inequality-200120-en.pdf?sequence=36&isAllowed=y.

26. ILO. (2018, June 28). *Care work and care jobs for the future of decent work.* Retrieved October 4, 2021, from https://www.ilo.org/global/publications/books/WCMS_633135/lang--en/index.html.

27. Grantham, K., Rouhani, L., Gupta, N., Melesse, M., Dhar, D., Kapoor Mehta, S., & Jha Kingra, K. (2021). (issue brief). *The Covid-19 Era: An Urgent Need for Change Evidence Review of the Global Childcare Crisis and The Road For Post-Covid-19 Recovery And Resilience.* The Gates Foundation. Retrieved October 4, 2021, from https://docs.gatesfoundation.org/documents/evidence_review_of_the_global_childcare_crisis_and_the_road_ahead_for_covid-19_recovery_and_resilience_english.pdf.

28. IMF. (2020, June 1). *World economic outlook update, June 2020: A crisis like no other, an uncertain recovery.* Retrieved October 4, 2021, from https://www.imf.org/en/Publications/WEO/Issues/2020/06/24/WEOUpdateJune2020.

29. Saraiva, C. (2021, March 9). *Women Could Give $20 Trillion Boost to Economic Growth by 2050.* Bloomberg.com. Retrieved October 4, 2021, from https://www.bloomberg.com/news/articles/2021-03-09/women-could-give-20-trillion-boost-to-economic-growth-by-2050.

30. Marcus Noland, Tyler Moran and Barbara Kotschwar, *Is Gender Diversity Profitable?*, Washington, D. C., Peterson Institute for International Economics, 2016, retrieved from, http://www.piie.com/system/files/documents/wp16-3.pdf.
31. McKinsey & Company, 2021.
32. Kunze & Miller, 2014.
33. Booth, Alison L., Marco Francesconi, and Jeff Frank (2003). "A Sticky Floors Model of Promotion, Pay, and Gender." European Economic Review 47(2): 295-322.
34. Matsa, David A. and Amalia R. Miller (2011). "Chipping Away at the Glass Ceiling: Gender Spillovers in Corporate Leadership." ***American Economic Review***, 101(3): 635–39.
35. Bell, Linda A. (2005). "Women-Led Firms and the Gender Gap in Top Executive Jobs." IZA Working Paper.
36 Working Mother Research Institute, *The Gender Gap at the Top*, June 2019, https://www.workingmother.com/sites/workingmother.com/files/attachments/2019/06/women_at_the_top_correct_size.pdf.
37. McKinsey & Company, *Women in the Workplace 2021*, September 29, 2021, https://www.mckinsey.com/featured-insights/diversity-and-inclusion/women-in-the-workplace.
38. K. Grantham, et al., *The COVID-19 Era: An Urgent Need for Change: Evidence Review of the Global Childcare Crisis and the Road for Post-COVID-19 Recovery and Resilience, 2021*, https://docs.gatesfoundation.org/documents/evidence_review_of_the_global_childcare_crisis_and_the_road_ahead_for_covid-19_recovery_and_resilience_english.pdf.
39. Herminia Ibarra, Nancy M. Carter, and Christine Silva, "Why Men Still Get More Promotions Than Women," *Harvard Business Review*, September 2010, 80–85.
40. R. H. Anderson and D. G. Smith, (2019, August 7). "What Men Can Do to Be Better Mentors and Sponsors to Women," *Harvard Business Review*, August 7, 2019, https://hbr.org/2019/08/what-men-can-do-to-be-bettermentors-and-sponsors-towomen#:~: text=Recent percent20research percent20from percent20the percent20Center,and percent20race percent20match percent20their percent20own.
41. See, for example, Hannah Riley Bowles, Linda Babcock, and Lei Lai, "Social Incentives for Gender Differences in the Propensity to Initiate Negotiations: Sometimes It Does Hurt to Ask," *Organizational Behavior and Human Decision Processes* 103.1 (May 2007): 84–103.
42. Carter and Silva; Sylvia Ann Hewlett, Kerrie Peraino, Laura Sherbin, and Karen Sumberg, The Sponsor Effect: Breaking Through the Last Glass Ceiling, *Harvard Business Review Research Report*, December 2010.
43. L. Joy, H. M. Wagner, and S. Narayanan, (2007, October 15). *The Bottom Line: Corporate Performance and Women's Representation on Boards*, Catalyst, October 15, 2007, https://www.catalyst.org/research/thebottom-line-corporate-performance-and-womens-representation-on-boards/.

Acknowledgements

We want to recognize the contribution that two key researchers have made to our work:

Kelly Reineke's Ph.D. dissertation on how power differences impact communication, and Deborah Tannen's many books on gender communication.

Maria Nalywayko was the first to partner with us on piloting the 12 Rules program through her ground- breaking Women In Leadership program at Core Logic.

The publishing team consisted of the valuable guidance provided by John Willig at Literary Services Inc., and Martha Bullen at Bullen Publishing Services.

We were thrilled to receive the cover and interior design from Christy Day and her team at Constellation Book Services, and the many practical tips from our editor Heather Rodino.

Big thanks to Bob Brandon and Sergio Barragan for giving us legal advice along the way.

We want to thank the 9 inspiring women who have shared their life and career journeys with us:

Dr. Marcela Del Carmen, Lisa Feiner, Srijana Karki, Susan Morris, Silvinia Moschini, Maria Nalywayko, Judith Obari, Ofra Strauss, and Liezl Tolentino.

Finally, we all know the book would never have been realized without the continual support and advice from Merry Cohen.

Thanks again to you all,

Mónica, Marty, Paula and Jovita

Other Books by Paula Santilli

El Poder de Poder, coauthored with Mónica Bauer and Marty Seldman
Empower You, Empower Her, coauthored with Mónica Bauer and
Marty Seldman

Other Books by Mónica Bauer

El Poder de Poder, coauthored with Paula Santilli and Marty Seldman
Empower You, Empower Her, coauthored with Paula Santilli and
    Marty Seldman

Other Books by Marty Seldman

Super Selling Through Self Talk
Performance Without Pressure
Survival of the Savvy, coauthored with Rick Brandon
Executive Stamina, coauthored with Joshua Seldman
Customer Tells, coauthored with John Futterknecht and Ben Sorensen
Leading in the Global Matrix, coauthored with John Futterknecht
El Poder de Poder, coauthored with Paula Santilli and Mónica Bauer
Empower You Empower Her, coauthored with Paula Santilli and
    Mónica Bauer

MÓNICA BAUER
VICE PRESIDENT, CORPORATE AFFAIRS, PEPSICO

MÓNICA BAUER is Vice President of Corporate Affairs for PepsiCo, the second-largest food & beverage company globally. She helps shape and execute the global Corporate Affairs strategy and the cultural agenda for the function.

Before this role, Mónica was VP, Corporate Affairs for PepsiCo Latin America.

In February 2020, she published the book *The Power of Empowerment: Women Building Latin America* with Paula Santilli, CEO of PepsiCo Latin America, and Marty Seldman, executive coach. The same authors published *Empowering You, Empowering Her* the year after.

Mónica earned her degree in International Relations at the Autonomous Technological Institute of Mexico (ITAM) and completed her MBA in the Instituto de Empresa in Madrid.

DR. MARTY SELDMAN
CHAIRMAN AND CO-FOUNDER, OPTIMUM ASSOCIATES

DR. MARTY SELDMAN is a corporate trainer, executive coach, and organizational psychologist. He received a B.A. in mathematics from Cornell University and completed his Ph.D. in clinical psychology at Temple University.

From 1972 to 1986, Marty specialized in the field of training. This experience included training trainers, designing training programs, and serving as VP of Sales for a training company. In 1986 he began his career as an executive coach and has become the coach of choice for many Fortune 500 companies. Marty has trained tens of thousands of executives around the globe through his seminars and coached over 2000 executives one-on-one. Approximately half of the executives Marty has coached are women, people of color, or non-U.S. executives.

Marty has written 9 books, including *Survival of the Savvy* (Free Press, 2004) which was a *Wall Street Journal* Best Seller, *Executive Stamina,* and his newest book, *A Woman's Guide to Power, Presence and Protection*, coauthored with Mónica Bauer, Paula Santilli and Jovita Thomas-Williams.

In addition to Marty's corporate work, he is active in the non-profit sector as a coach and consultant. He also serves on the boards of four organizations that work in the areas of human rights and poverty alleviation.

PAULA SANTILLI
CEO, PEPSICO LATIN AMERICA

PAULA SANTILLI is the chief executive officer of PepsiCo Latin America, leading the company's food and beverage businesses for Mexico, South America, Central America, and the Caribbean. She is responsible for over $7 billion in annual net revenue. Besides being a member of PepsiCo's Executive Committee, she previously served as the president of PepsiCo Mexico Foods (PMF), where she also led the PepsiCo Mexico Foundation.

Prior to this, she was the chief operating officer (COO) of all business units of PepsiCo Mexico Foods, providing leadership for Sales, Marketing and Operations. Additionally, as COO, Paula helped guide strategy and played a leadership role in talent development for the business. Her ample experience also encompasses managing the savory and beverages business in Mexico and leadership roles in Foods and Snacks in the Latin America Southern Cone region, including Argentina, Uruguay and Paraguay.

Before joining PepsiCo, Paula worked for Campbell's Soups and Kellogs's in Argentina in marketing roles. Moreover, Paula has been a strong champion of Diversity and Inclusion, increasing women's representation in Mexico. She won the Catalyst Practices Recognition in New York in 2014 and was included in Fortune's 50 Most Powerful Women International list. Besides this, she is a sponsor of the Inspira Program in Latin America, which seeks to propel female executive development within the business. Paula holds a degree in Communications and Advertising Sciences from University of Salvador in Buenos Aires and a postgraduate degree in Marketing and International Studies from Miami University of Ohio.

JOVITA THOMAS-WILLIAMS, SPHR, GPHR,
MASSACHUSETTS GENERAL HOSPITAL

JOVITA THOMAS-WILLIAMS is the Senior Vice President of Human Resources at Massachusetts General Hospital (MGH) and the Massachusetts General Physicians Organization (MGPO) in Boston, MA. Massachusetts General Hospital is a member of the Mass General Brigham HealthCare System, an 80,000 employee, $13.5 billion integrated not-for-profit academic health system founded by Brigham and Women's Hospital and Massachusetts General Hospital, and a teaching affiliate of Harvard Medical School. She joined MGH from Yale New Haven Hospital, in New Haven, CT, where she served as the Vice President of Human Resources. Her HR leadership experience spans decades and a variety of industries—including healthcare, higher education, consumer products, manufacturing, hospitality & entertainment, and management consulting—across North and South America and Europe.

As a senior HR executive, Jovita is widely known for successfully balancing the strategic needs of prestigious Fortune 100 employers and academic medical centers while remaining a strong advocate for employees and fostering workplace environments where employees feel valued, supported, and, most of all, heard. She was recognized among the 2021 most impactful Black Women in Boston.

A native of Detroit, MI, Jovita holds a Bachelor of Science degree from Tuskegee Institute and earned both her MBA and MILR (Master in Industrial & Labor Relations) at Cornell University (first in university history). Additionally, she is the recipient of both the SPHR and GPHR professional certifications. Jovita takes great pride in her career accomplishments but considers her most cherished role as that of mother to her beloved son — the center of her universe.

Made in the USA
Columbia, SC
07 February 2022

55184330R00104